From the Desert to the Lakes

From the Desert
to the Lakes

Four South Australian Aboriginal Memoirs

From the Desert to the Lakes: Four South Australian Aboriginal Memoirs
ISBN 978 1 76041 531 0
Copyright © individual authors 2018
Cover photo of Lake Alexandrina: Matthew Summerton [CC BY-SA 3.0
(https://creativecommons.org/licenses/by-sa/3.0)], via Wikimedia Commons

First published separately by Nyiri Publications
Wendy Harris: A Coober Pedy Pioneer (2006)
I Had a Good Life – It Was Beautiful (2008)
Outback Heart (2010)
You Have To Survive Somehow (2011)

This combined volume first published 2018 by
GINNINDERRA PRESS
PO Box 3461 Port Adelaide 5015
www.ginninderrapress.com.au

Contents

A Coober Pedy Pioneer	Wendy Harris	7
I Had a Good Life – It Was Beautiful	Totty (Harriet) Rankine	33
Outback Heart	Audrey Wonga	67
You Have To Survive Somehow	Brian Strangways	95
Thanks		133

Kulinma. Wiya tjutaya nyiri nyangangka ngaranyi ka nyura alara nyakula tjinguru ngalturingkuku munu kuntaringkuku.

Please listen. Be aware that some people in this book have passed away and, on opening it and seeing them, you might be sad and sorry.

A Coober Pedy Pioneer

Wendy Harris
(Yankunytjatjara)

Dedicated to my poor blind Kami – my grandmother – Unkari.

People don't believe me

People don't believe me – nothing – that I was there in Coober Pedy a long time ago. I was born in 1932 at Larry Well, Alpanyinta, and I was very little when my uncle, Uncle Pantju, and my aunty, Imangatja, brought me down to Coober Pedy with a five camels. He was going to sell that five camels. No cars in those days. There was no field here in Coober Pedy – there was only one man digging a hole, I remember. I think he was a German bloke. This is a long time ago!

We was living in the dugout – the dugout, by the water tank. Yes, I was with my uncle – Uncle Punch (Pantju) Gibson – my mother's brother, living in the dugouts by the water tank. Then the uncle sell his camels and gone back to take his wife back to Ernabella – she belonged at Ernabella. He took me back and put me into mother – at Wintinna, I think.

That was after my father passed away.

Living as a family at Alpanyinta

My *ngunytju*, my mother, and my *mama*, father, were living in a station, Alpanyinta, Larry Well, next door to Sailors Well. It's a long time ago. They were all right there and we lived together as a family. My sister's name was Dolly. (Now it's Dolly Ramsen and she has her homeland at Tjiwuru, right out from Ernabella.) My sister and I had a second name as well – that was our nickname. Mine was 'Baby'.

My father was the boss of Larry Well. He used to have somebody working for him – but in those days we didn't know who he was.

My mother's name was Maggie Marousen. I can't pronounce her second name – her *Anangu*, Aboriginal, name. It was Ngupulya. She was already married to my father and carried his name – George Kimberley Marousen. My father was uncle of the other George

*Wendy Harris, aged 18, at the River Torrens, Adelaide. 1950.
'Joycie Wilson – Archie Badenoch's sister – and me were having lunch
and a man came and took the photos.'
(Wendy Harris private collection)*

Kimberley Marousen, the one who lived in Coober Pedy. That was his nephew – and they had the same name.

My father was the same colour or a bit lighter than me. He was an Afghan. He had a wagon, he had a two-seater jinker and he had horses and he had camels. He had all them! I don't know how many camels – might be ten or twenty camels. Too many camels! And horses – one for my mother, one for my dad, one for me, one for my sister.

We had nanny goats – a lot. Me and my sister used to go and milk the nanny goats. We used to go under the nanny goats' legs and grab them by the tit and drink it. We couldn't get hold of it so we used to knock down the nanny goats and then lay down and drink the milk. Instead of milking them! Oh dear, oh dear!

Sometimes we used to get up and fight with one another and pull one another's hair for that goat. And the goat used to kick us and send us going. We used to cry – both of us – and run away. We'd go for another goat when we finished crying. Cranky! Two cranky ones – I don't know! Cranky isn't in it!

We had a little built-in shack at Alpanyinta with an army tent in it as well. And a shed – *wiltja* shed – to go outside and sit or lay down when the summer comes, you know, like a shade. That was our house. We used to stay in that house at Alpanyinta all the time. We never used to go anywhere.

But I used to run away to the sandhills. Blue bushes were up in the red sandhills. We used to get behind the blue bushes and I used to steal a book from my father's tent and run away with the book – hide away. It was a nice, pretty book to look at and I used to run away by myself and sing out for my sister. Up in the sandhills. She used to run up. We can't read but we used to look at all the pretty pictures. They were some sort of old station pictures. We used to fight like cats and dogs over that book.

They couldn't find us. And then they find us and you know what? I make trouble for my *ngunytju*, my mother. Any time I used to do wrong, my father used to belt my mother with a whip. Poor thing!

He was a cruel man. That's why my mother sent him going. He used to stock whip her all the time when everything go wrong – when the kids do wrong.

There were a lot of *Anangu*, Aboriginal, living out at the camp – a long way, about two miles from my father's home by the well. They'd come in getting water, a drum of water now and then. Up and down. My uncle (Eileen Crombie's father) and Eileen Crombie's mother used to come in too, come in to the camp to get a feed or to get tea, damper, sugar (you know, at that time they was getting that) and do a little bit of job for my father round the place.

I remember Eileen Crombie and Eileen Brown too. When I was a little kid I used to chase them around. Eileen Brown used to work for my father: cleaning up or sweeping up, boiling up the water or tea. My father paid her with food and she'd go back every day to the camp. Poor thing!

We didn't know English. My *kamuru*, my uncle, Pantju, used to understand English. He used to talk English. He used to repeat all the Aboriginal language words in English. He used to help us and all the dark womans that were with us – all the O'Tooles, Marousens, Russells too, back there at Alypanyinta, Larry Well.

There used to be Russells a bit further up the station living: Russells (old George Russell), O'Tooles, Marousen whitefellas. All the *kungkas*, all the womans, used to go with white fellas in those days when I was born. One goes with that white one, one goes with that white one...

Larry O'Toole and my father used to be friends. He was Irish. They used to go with the camels' pack and go for it – get the sugar and tea and flour... They could have been going to Oodnadatta picking it up. They used to get a lot there. Some of the relations used to go and ask my father for tea, sugar and flour and he used to go off to Oodnadatta and bring it back.

Many years later… Uncle Pantju Gibson with Ngitji Ngitji Mona Turr, addressing the capacity crowd at the Adelaide Town Hall meeting to oppose the radioactive dump, November 1999. (Photo courtesy of Fernando M. Gonçalves, Avante Media)

Left alone

Then my mama, my father, got sick and was dying so they sent him to Oodnadatta on a truck – a big red truck – and they put him half dying in a cot, a big cot like a baby's. We were standing around there looking, saying goodbye to Dad. Mum was telling us kids standing around saying goodbye to him – 'Kiss him.' We were only little ones. They put him up and he left us there. We was left alone ourself that night with our mother.

They must have buried him at Wellbourne Hill on the way to Oodnadatta or in Oodnadatta. When I went there to Oodnadatta, there was no burial there – his name wasn't there. They usually buried them on the way. Lots of people died on the road – and they buried them on the way to some places. They don't put the name on them. I'm never going to find the burial for him.

Billy Giles was the boss of Wellbourne Hill but his son Ernie Giles, the boss after his father, is gone now – he shift. But Bradman Russell, Eileen Crombie's big brother, is living in Marla Bore. He used to carry me round when I was a little girl. He's there today in Marla Bore, Eileen told me. He knows where they put him.

Then we saw one fellow with his country western clothes – Dickie Cullinan. he took over. Well, we thought he was going to take over. He came over that morning and he went into my father's tent and took all the food, all the tins of fruit and everything – the tent and the whole thing. He stuck it in his truck. But he left us half the food stuff – the tins that father left for our mother. Then he went straight on.

He was a tall fellow – well, he looked like tall to me then. Really, he was about the same size as his son today – Johnny Cullinan – not that tall at all. He had Wallatinna Station. He was married to a black woman too, that fella: a short, fat *kungka*. He had a dark woman with him that time. Fat *kungka* she was – short, fat woman. He had a white woman but he was going with the black woman, sneaky way. My mother knows him but my mother not here. When I was fifteen in Umeewarra Mission, she died. She died in Oodnadatta working for the police. She died of measles – bad measles, she had. *Ngaltutjara* – poor thing.

Moving around with the family

But after my *mama*, my father, died, Alpanyinta (Larry Well) finished. Nobody lived there after that. We went out, we went away into the bush where the other camping place was. Everybody was camping there. It was the main place.

Most of the time after that we went to Wintinna. We was living there down the creek in the wurleys. From there we scattered out looking for tucker. Mother was working there. Taking the nanny goats out. We'd stay there a little while – a month maybe at Mount Willoughby: Wintinna, Wellbourne Hill, Mount Willoughby – all that line; my *ngunytju*, my mother, and me and my sister. We was all the time up in those stations up there shifting camps. I knew the bush inside out and the stations too.

We used to live with our family then, Unkari and Tjungura, on Wintinna Station, all their families there: *kamuru tjuta*, uncles; *kuntili tjuta*, uncles' wives; and *tjitji tjuta*, children. We used to live all there – all of us families altogether at the stations. We didn't have grandfathers. We don't know our grandfathers. Only our grandmothers was still alive. I was the main one looking after *Unkari*, the blind grandmother, all that time – a little kid like me looking after her – when she was blind there. Don't know how I did it! I did it somehow 'cause God told me to. She was blind – I had to look after her when I was a little kid! Anybody can't do that – I was the first one.

Cook for her; wash the clothes for her; wash her body for her in the tub. (She was fat and I couldn't lift her up; she had to get out somehow herself.) Then put clean clothes on – everything. I loved my *kami*, my grandmother, and I looked after her well in the stations. She was blind. I still remember it. I was broken-hearted when the policeman took me away. And I had to leave her behind. I lived with her in the stations.

Heading to Coober Pedy

Then my mother brought me down to Coober Pedy. We travelled from Mount Willoughby with Aunty Linda Brown and Uncle Paddy Brown. They were travelling to go with us back to Coober Pedy. They were two sisters: my mother and Linda Brown (Umatji) were two sisters, sisters *Anangu*, Aboriginal way. Their mothers – Unkari and Tjungara – were two sisters whitefella way. Yes, my grandmother, Unkari, was sister to that O'Toole – *ulkumunu*, old woman – Sammy Brown's grandmother. Her *Anangu* name was Tjungara.

That's where we settled for a while – in Coober Pedy. We were living on the Flat – no houses then, no nothing there. We was living in the wurley – yes, we put up a *wiltja* for ourselves. Me and my sister, we was running around naked. Eileen Wingfield was here – a *kungkawara*, big teenager – on her camel with a load of materials, cottons and needles and scissors and everything to make a dress. We was naked. She saw us running around naked and my *ngunytju*, my mother, bought some of

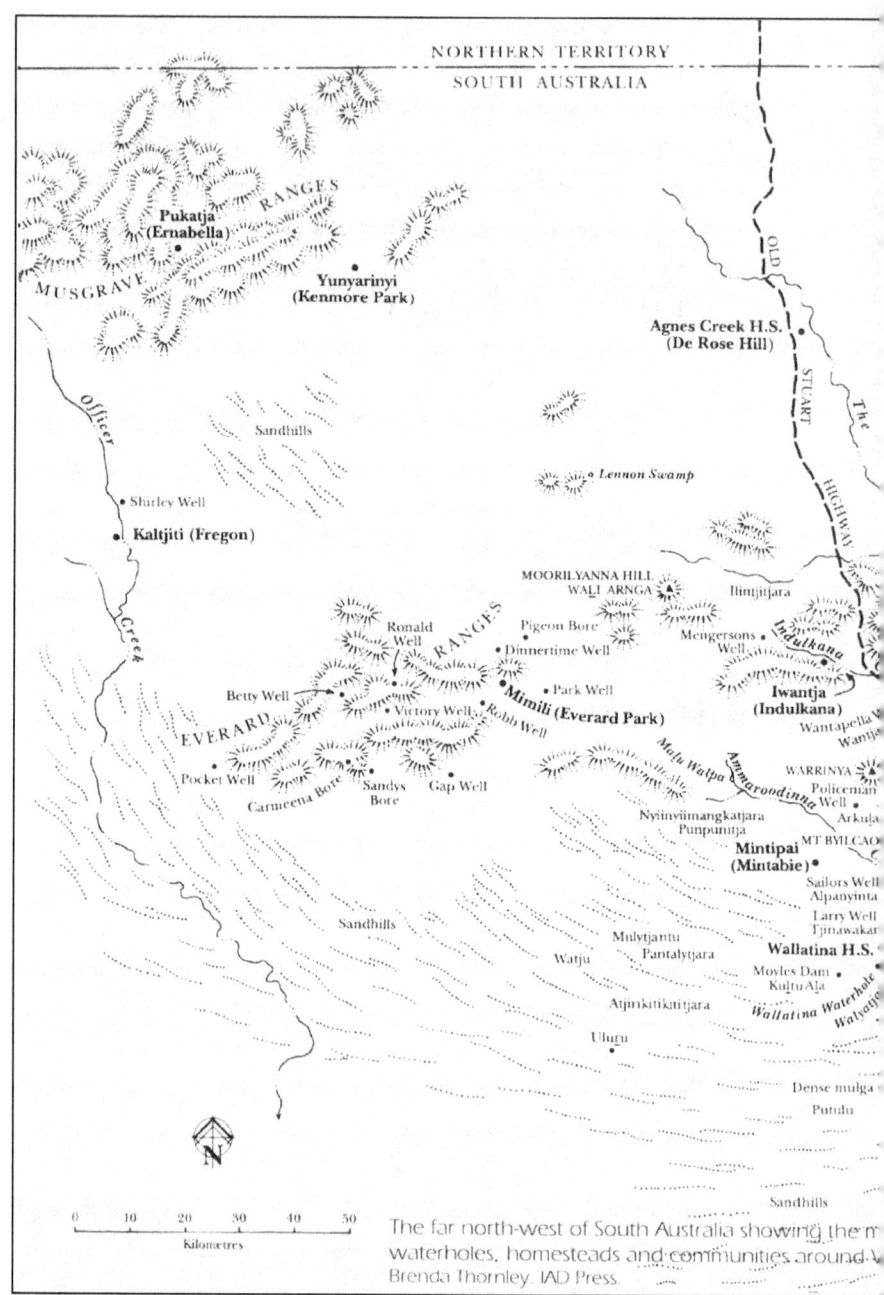

The far north-west of South Australia showing the waterholes, homesteads and communities around. Brenda Thornley. IAD Press.

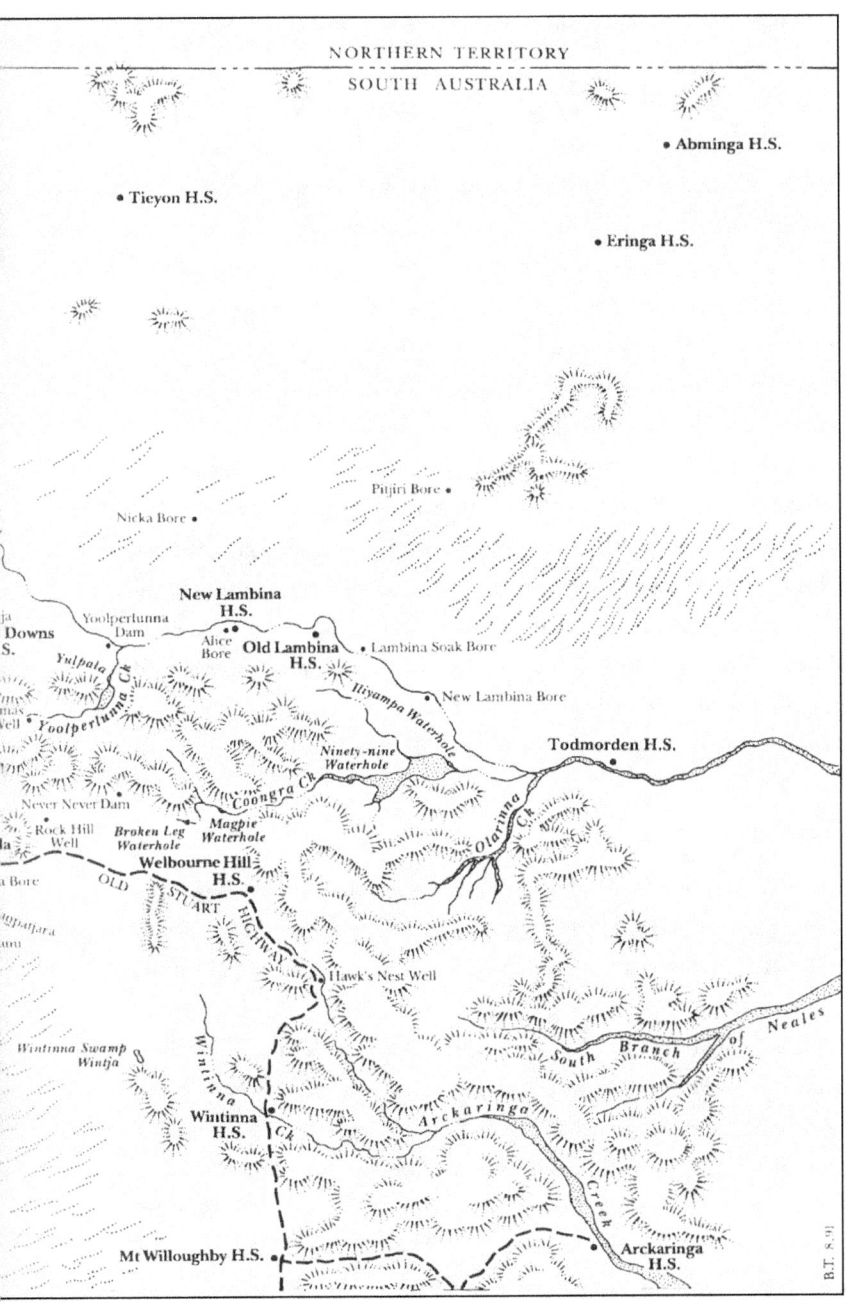

the material. Eileen made the dress and put the dress on us and we was dressed straight away.

We lived in Coober Pedy for a while that time. We were altogether with our family. We stayed down the Flat, looking for opal. On the top of the ground we looked for opal – there was plenty. I was older, my sister Dolly was younger. I was about eight or nine years old. I remember Emily Austin's father, Jim Lennon – Ka_ti_ti Lennon – was here too buying opal from us little kids and giving us apples and oranges, hoping we could find the opal on the ground. We were galloping around looking for the opal. Apples and oranges we were selling it for. That was a long time ago but I remember it.

There were only two or three *A_n_angu* there on the Flat that I remember: Jessie Brown and Billy Brown when they was little. We was all together, playing in the Flat. Tutjili was Jessie's grandfather, I think – his whitefella name was Louie. He used to live in Mount Willoughby Station. I forget the woman's name now. Jessie and Billy Brown, their grandchildren, lived with them. They'd come over and see Coober Pedy and go back again to Mount Willoughby. We kept on going for opal and then we went back too.

Taken away

Yes, we went back to Mount Willoughby again. We lived down the creek at Mount Willoughby – with the wurley. We stayed in Mount Willoughby. After that we went to Blue Barnard, behind Wintinna, close to Cadney Park.

That's where we mixed up with Eileen Crombie's mob. We stayed in their camp. Eileen Crombie is a long way younger than me. I was up walking around at Alpanyinta when she was just born. Eileen Crombie's father, Peter Russell, was the brother to my mother so I call Eileen *kangku_r_u*, older sister, because her father is older than my mother. He was born in Fregon. (Uncle Pantju – Uncle Punch – was born in Amata. He was their other brother again.)

That's where we went – to Blue Barnard – and stayed there and the policeman took me away from there. 'Half-caste' kids, you know – they took away the 'half-caste' kids. I remember that one. I was the only one 'half-caste' kid they – the police – took from the stations. They took me away and took my *ngunytju*, my mother…

My mother was going to work in the Oodnadatta police station. That was before I was taken to Port Augusta. We headed for Oodnadatta. I was in the Home in Oodnadatta and they sent me on the train to Port Augusta with my eyes – I had bad eyes. I had to go because of my eyes. And from there they put me in the hospital when I got to Port Augusta. I was in hospital for I don't know how many weeks I was in hospital. They took care of me – they had to wash my eyes and brush my eyes and turn my eyes right way, for the crooked eyes.

My sister Dolly used to look after the blind grandmother, Unkari, after that. The police told her to stay at the camp and look after her. Poor old grandmother. I loved my *kami*, my grandmother, and I looked after her well in the stations. Broken-hearted when the policeman took me away to leave her behind. That was to never return.

I didn't come back. I didn't see her since. I wish I didn't have to leave her that time. I wish I didn't have to go. She died fretting for me. I was fretting for her.

In the Home

And after that, they couldn't find where I was living. They couldn't find it so they put me straight in the Port Augusta Mission Home at Umeewarra – and that's where they put me. It must have been 1940 – some year like that when the war was on – that I went to Umeewarra Mission. I went to the Mission for one and a half years. I learnt to read there. Linda Dingaman used to come to Umeewarra Mission to visit me. We had the same father, different mothers. The women shared the man but we didn't all live together. We keep to the right skin. (Whitefellas are different. They come from overseas and just marry anyone.)

At Umeewarra, in the Mission there, Miss Cantle and Miss Simmonds and Miss Morton, the Sister, that's all that was there. Poor

At Umeewarra Mission (now Davenport Community). From left: Wendy Marousen, May Hiel, Elsie Reid, Alvis Dingaman, Betty Lang, Gwen Starkey. 'They older than me, that lot. I was only a little tacker.'
(Wendy Harris private collection)

old thing, Miss Morton – she's a good one: the one with the medicine, the tablets. There was Reids – Colin Reid, Yakky Reid, Pinda, Frank Reid, all them was there; Wingfields – Billy Wingfield was there;

Wendy Marousen with baby Frankie Lovegrove.
(Wendy Harris private collection)

Starkeys – Gwennie Starkey was there, Lorna Starkey, Stanley Starkey; Davises; Dingamans. They was all in Umeewarra Mission. That was a long time ago! They was all at Umeewarra. That's the first lot I've been with. That was a long time ago.

Frankie Lovegrove – that's the one I was holding in my arms as a baby. I got the photo here somewhere. I've got the photos. That was the first lot.

Then there was the second lot of kids at Umeewarra. There was a lot of kids: Archie Badenoch (that was really a Brown), Archie Brown, Ivy Ross, Clarice Ross. Alvis Dingaman: she's the one that learnt me English when she was a tiny little girl running around. I never used to talk English; I only talked language before. I didn't understand a word of English. Myall I was – no English! A real bush girl! I don't know how I talked to my father – we just talked to our mother, that's all. He must have understood.

We used to go for school in the Mission Home. Miss Cantle and Miss Simmonds were the teachers: Miss Simmonds in the morning, Miss Cantle teaches in the afternoon. After dinner she comes on. Sometimes they sick or tired and help one another and she takes it on in the morning too. That was long years ago. I must have been eleven or twelve or thirteen. I only learned to read a little bit – easy words. Yes, I only went to Bible reading and school for one and a half years.

They were looking after the babies in the Mission Home. They put me off from school and made me stay home and do the housework – changing babies' napkins, washing *kuna* nappies and things like that. Setting tables for dinner, serving dinner – waitress, changing tables: all that I used to do. Cleaning tables, polishing floors in the dining room where there's going to be dinner. Bathing babies, feeding babies, putting them to sleep – the whole lot. I was keeping going from that at the Home learning everything they put me in. I wasn't learning in the school – I was learning at the Home everything they put me in. And when I turned fifteen, when I learned all that, they sent me out to work. I had to learn – that's why I knew everything in my job.

Put to work

I ended up at Sheringa Station, between Port Lincoln and Streaky Bay, near Elliston – along that line. A long way. There were stores in Elliston – shops in Elliston.

I was working there then. Doing all sort of jobs. They had sheep and bullocks and *tjuki tjukis*, chooks, on that station. I worked there when I was fifteen. I went over there and worked there. When I turned sixteen, I worked a little bit more. Then during seventeen, Mrs

Johnston from the station got sorry for me because I had nobody and no fun – a young girl like myself working all the time in that station. So she sent me to Adelaide.

Married life

I lived in Adelaide when I was seventeen, eighteen, nineteen. When I was nineteen, I met someone. He was in the navy in the Second World War. He win that war and finished in the navy. Then he was a soldier in the army, training cadets for the Third World War – if that happens. It wasn't on yet at that time.

Then he met me, got discharged from the army and married me. He was born in May 1918, so he was a long way older than me. Came back to the station – Sheringa Station – having the wedding there. Yes, I got married to him – James Stewart Patrick Harris, my husband – Wendy and Glenys and Yvonne's father. We had four girls. One girl we lost in the middle between Yvonne and Wendy. She was very little – just born, a month old or something. I was carrying her when I was twenty or nineteen and she would be fifty-three years old now, *ngaltutjara*, poor thing.

Then I finished with my husband. He was carrying on getting drunk. He didn't hit me or the little ones but he was so drunk I was frightened, frightened that he could have hit the little ones. I was told to leave him because my health was not too good. I had to leave him because of my nerves. I was looking after two little ones, three little ones, four little ones...

And now I can't find Yvonne. I gave her to Mrs Johnston when she was two years old. Saw her when she was ten years old. She was in Mr Cameron's school in the radio correspondence – Sheringa Station. What could I do? I was too busy working. The Welfare told me to go to work and they put the kids in some home – a foster home. Sister McKenzie was the welfare woman and Mr Penhall, he was the boss. They took my kids and I was too young to speak for myself. I had to go to work. They found me a job in Clare in the laundry – laundress.

In those days, Welfare was taking their way. Not because we was bad. The husband was drinking. They couldn't give us any money. I had to go and work but I missed 'em very much, those kids. Those kids, the girls, were with English people.

Looking for where I belonged

Then I finished with that work and I wanted to go back to Coober Pedy – or to Port Augusta at least. Eileen Crombie with her first husband, Billy Pepper, brought me back from Port Augusta to Coober Pedy to work there. I came back. I got off the train from Adelaide in Port Augusta looking for where I belonged.

I knew these two – Syddie and Tilly Waye – straight away on the lawn there. I went back and stayed with them at Davenport – on the Mission.

My *kangkuru*, my sister Eileen Crombie, was in Port Augusta. She knew she had to pick me up somewhere. She came to visit me there and cried her eyes out. She said, 'You don't know where you belong. Just come back and see Coober Pedy.'

On the lawn, Gladstone Square, Port Augusta.
From left to right: Wendy Harris, little Syd Waye, Syddie Waye, Tilly Waye.
'Came off the train at Port Augusta to go to Coober Pedy to be working at Brewsters.'
(Wendy Harris private collection, used with permission of Emily Munyungka Austin)

Coober Pedy, 1964.
(Photo and named locations courtesy of the Traeger family)

Then she carried me on to Coober Pedy. I came home looking for the people I'd left behind.

At Kingoonya when we got off the train from Port Augusta, I was sleeping on the ground.

I said, 'No, I don't want to sleep on the ground. I want to go to the pub to sleep.' I was a fussy poor little thing – I was taken away when I was young.

But Eileen Crombie said, 'No, we've got to sleep out in the bush tonight for the time being to get the mail truck to go to Coober Pedy.'

Some whitefella was driving the mail truck at that time – when I was twenty-six years old. They were carrying petrols and all that and the passengers and their luggage to go to Coober Pedy. We were just sitting on the back there on the swags and things, our bags and our cases.

Pioneer's head waitress

Yes, my *kangku̱ru*, my sister Eileen Crombie, brought me back to work there in Coober Pedy. We was working at the roadhouse for the road travellers. In summer time, they run with their caravans. We was setting the tables, waiting on the tables. Some had to make beds. (They come for beds in the night time.) That was when the first Pioneer bus started. I was head waitress, mind you! For a long while!

Pioneer bus coming into Coober Pedy. Background: Brewster's Road House. (Photograph courtesy of State Library of South Australia and Roger Pedrotta – B6422)

Next to the rest room, on the right where Ampol used to be, was Jack and Edna Brewster's shop. That's where we used to work. We was all black ones there; might be one white one working. Pioneers first and then Murray Valley Coaches we used to serve. They used to keep running up and down all the time to Coober Pedy. And I used to teach young ones – Shirley Williams was one that I learned how to set the table.

'Put the plate down on the right-hand side. Take it away – the dirty one – on the left-hand side.'

All that rubbish!

We had a lot, a lot, a lot of tips – a whole handful of money we had. I used to take it in the kitchen and share it out with the cooks; with the girls that make the beds, change the dirty sheets and make it. Oh, we had a good time. Still, I learnt to do a lot of things like that. Full sometimes – bus full! Fifty-five to sixty-five people. And then we'd start again for the next bus – fifty-five again. All that line on the way down. And on top of that fifty-seven come along again! And seventy-six. And we'd have to reset it quick! Run around!

I used to be the one on my feet all the time. Wheww! Lots of them used to come through. Ride up and down all the time. They used to love us very much – drivers and all. The first Pioneers running through and I was a Pioneer – light blue and white Pioneer.

There were seven of us girls. We used to get up at five o'clock to get up, have a shower to get ready. There were three in the kitchen, two in the dining room, two out making beds.

It was a hard job but I took it right or wrong. On my feet all the time. Never got a reference out of that or badge to remember something. We should have got a bonus for that – serving Pioneers. We had a good job, I'll tell you – nice!

We were the first Pioneers there and I was the Pioneers' head waitress. The Pioneers' colour was light blue and I had a lovely pale blue uniform, and lavender earrings and cardigan, and pantyhose and black shoes. I used to look lovely!

Working back and forth

I was walking up and down from the water tank. There was a camp over there. Houses too down at the water tank. I was staying up by the water tank with Roy and Betty Smith. Summer time I used to walk down to where Brewster's shop was. Jack and Mrs Brewster retired after that, poor things, and they were going to send us to Ayers Rock and we said, 'No. We stay here.'

All the time we was working for the Reserve then, cleaning up the

Matron of Honour. From left: best man Roy Smith, groom Henry O'Toole, bride Beverley O'Toole (nee Smith), matron of honour Wendy Harris. (Photo courtesy of the Traeger family)

On the Reserve. 'I was working right there in the shed.'
(Photo courtesy of the Traeger family)

houses and offices and things down at the Reserve. They gave us a job down the Reserve then, washing clothes for the old people.

Old Pastor Traeger was there but the washing boss was Shirley. There were a whole lot of washing machines there at the shed. I was there for a long time – washing the school clothes too. *Ngunytju tjuṯa*, the mothers, used to wash them and we used to wash the old clothes.

I had no kids still. They were in some English people's home. They were together some of the time. Yvonne was with Mrs Johnston. I was also working at the hospital, there in the old hospital. And even before that in the maternity in the Bush Hospital. I was a cleaner and laundress, washing floors in the maternity, to make the bed where the *kungka tjuṯa*, the ladies, lay down and have their babies. And sterilising bandages. Sister White was there in the Bush Hospital.

I went back and forth, you know. If they wanted help from the hospital, I went back to the hospital. Then I went back to the Reserve. They give me a job there. I was living on the Reserve. I had a little house there when I was working.

And that's the way I end. That's my story.

Old memories

Yes, I knew Milly Tayor, Emily Austin, Tilly Waye – three sisters; and Lallie Lennon. The big ones, *kungkawara tjuta*, I used to run around with. I knew them since childhood. They know me too. They was up there with me at Alpanyinta, playing around in the sandhills. I used to chase them up – sticky beak to see where they were going. I used to be the one chasing them around. Cranky! They used to put me in the camel's back and used to buck me off. I used to cry and throw a stone and yell at them in my language, Yankunytjatjara.

And my mother and their mothers be behind the trees from us and we used to peep through the trees – they used to sing songs. They used to dance *inma* in the bush with the *kungka tjuta*, with all the other womans. It was all a long time ago but I remember it.

Coober Pedy 1964. Coober Pedy had become a township in 1958 when Wendy Harris 'went back to work there' (at Brewsters).
(Photo courtesy of the Traeger family)

Umoona Aged Care, Coober Pedy. Celebrating the victory over the radioactive dump, 2004. Eileen Brown dancing Inma. From left: Eileen Kampakuta Brown, Wendy Harris, Eileen Unkari Crombie, Michele Madigan. (Photo courtesy of Nina and Clare Brown, Irati Wanti archive)

The next generations. Wendy, Glenys and Yvonne with their families. (Wendy Harris private collection)

Word list

Yankunytjatjara	English
Anangu	Aboriginal person
inma	traditional dance
kami	grandmother
kamuru	mother's brother, 'uncle'
kamuru tjuta	uncles
kangkuru	older sister
kanku	shade, shelter, bush dwelling
kapi	water, rain
kuna	poo, faeces
kungka	woman
kungka tjuta	women (plural)
kungkawara (Pitjantjatjara word)	young teenage girl
kungkawara tjuta	young teenage girls
kuntili tjuta	father's sisters, uncles' wives
mama	father, father's brother, daddy
ngaltutjara	poor thing, dear one,
ngunytju	mother, mother's sister, mummy
tjitji tjuta	children
tjuki-tjuki (from the English)	chooks
ulkumunu (from the English)	old woman
wiltja (Pitjantjatjara word)	shade, shelter, bush dwelling

Reference

Goddard, Cliff (compiler). *Pitjantjatjara/Yankunytjatjara Dictionary.* IAD Press. Alice Springs. 1997.

Notes

On language
Wendy Harris remains fluent in her own language – Yankunyjatjara.

For her story, she uses just a few language words, including some which *Anangu* frequently use while speaking English.

On Aboriginal English as a recognised language: 'Aboriginal English has been maintained as a distinct variety of English because it is particularly suited to embodying what indigenous people want to say to one another, in an indigenous context adapting and using English to express an indigenous world view.' Ian G. Malcolm. *Language and Communication Enhancement for Two-way Education*. 1995.

On family relationship terms
Anangu usually use relationship terms when addressing each other including to brothers and sisters. Wendy refers to her (younger) sister-cousin, Eileen Crombie, as *kangkuru*, older sister, because Eileen's father is older than Wendy's mother.

Anangu refer to first cousins 'whitefella way' as brothers and sisters.

On location (see map, p. 16–17)
The Larry Well/Sailor's Well area is between Mintabie and Wallatinna Station (left centre lower section of map). Wendy Harris refers to both these areas as Alpanyinta.

The road shown is the old Stuart Highway. It went from station homestead to station homestead. The present highway was not surveyed and completed until the 1980s, on a more direct route.

Oodnadatta (off map) is about 210 kilometres west of Alpanyinta. Coober Pedy (off map) is about 250 kilometres to the south-east along the Stuart Highway.

The Reserve: in Coober Pedy, the Aboriginal Reserve later became Umoona Community. The early 1960s photograph (p. 28) shows the administration/working plant in the foreground with the original tin houses in the background.

I Had a Good Life – It Was Beautiful

Totty (Harriet) Rankine
(Ngarrindjeri)

nakari, black duck, my *ngaitji*

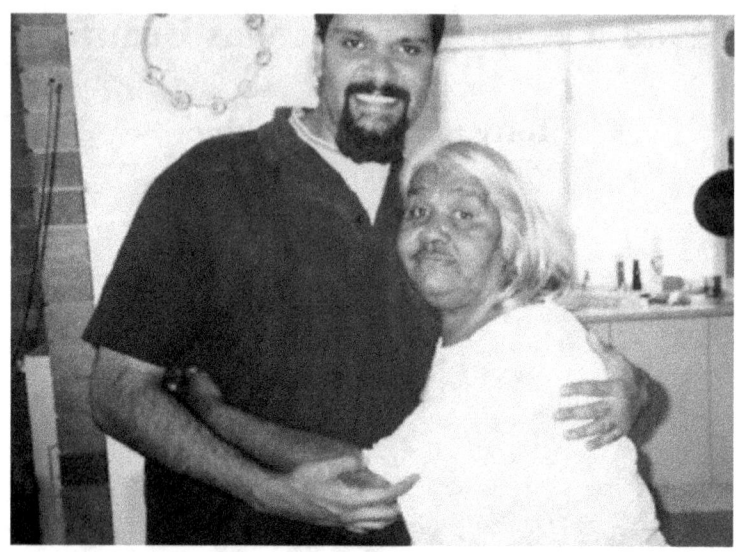

Dedicated to my only son, Anthony von Doussa Rankine.
(I thought I'd outlast him but my son beat me to the draw.)

Also to my beautiful daughter Nellie,
and to my grandchildren Leah, Anthony and Tanayha.

(Photos from the family's personal collection)

We were really off-the-land people

I can't grumble about anything when we was kids.

My dad, Hendle Rankine, used to go shooting – ducks. He used to come home with six or seven ducks. Beautiful! We were really off-the-land people, which was deadly, 'cause a lot of fellas didn't like ducks and fish and all of that.

'Cause we used to go along the Lake to get fish – *thukari* and all. Yes, we went fishing and all. Dad used to take us. He had two carts – two horses and two carts – and we used to go down to the sandy track. Then you go over past Big Hill then go down to Teringe, fishing: Teringe, that's down from Raukkan. We go down to the Lake, Lake Alexandrina.

I mean, we had everything! We used to go down to the bank. Lovely lines we used to have. And worms. We used to have those old lines first, made of cord. We used to have that for a line and we used to stretch it. We'd tie it to a fence or something and stretch it. Leave it for a couple of days or nearly a week… But it was lovely, *inna*?

And that used to be beautiful because Mum used to make damper 'cause the sand was lovely and clean for the damper when it was summer time – you know, not too hot. And it's lovely because it's warm and everything down there. We had nine kids in my dad and mum's family. Them lot in the photo – them five, they all lived: Polly, Leah, Henry, me, Sidney. Only Henry, me and Sidney left today. Fred, Hendle, Verlaine and George was the other four. Verlaine died when she was a baby. Fred was three or four. And George, I think George was a baby too.

There was such a lot of sorrows in our family.

I was born on Raukkan – known then as Point McLeay. Born on 6/6/1943. I think I was born in the hospital there on Raukkan – I hope so… Sidney was born in July 1955.

From the top clockwise: Sidney, Polly, Harriet (Totty), Henry, Leah. Mum (standing left) and Dad in centre.

Martha Rankine. Henry Rankine.
(Photos from the family's personal collection)

We all used to sleep in the bed together, even Margaret, Aunty Harriet's daughter; she used to always stay with us. There used to be Polly, Leah, me, Margie, Sidney, Henry… Big queen-size bed we used to have. Oh, I enjoyed it!

And sometimes I used to stay with Margie's Mum. Because of Mum having Freddy and Maxwell and Sidney after me, I used to live with Margaret's Mum – Aunty Harriet. 'Cause that's who I'm named after. I'm Harriet Agnes; my mother named me after my two aunties. Aunty Aggie Rigney was Dad's cousin. So soon as my son Tony and Stella found out they had a girl, it was Leah after my sister. Leah's name was Leah Winifred. My brother Sidney's named after Mum's and them's Uncle Sidney.

Aunty Harriet used to help Mum out a lot and I used to go and stay with her. Then she had Margie, so me and Margie sort of grew up together.

Nana Polly (née Beck) Long carrying Aunty Harriet with my mother, Annie, standing alongside. (Photo from the family's personal collection)

That's why me and Marg (Crompton she is now) – are sisters. Ye-es! That's my baby sister, I always call her. Her mum used to have a one little room house up with the township – up on Raukkan. Our house was down the Lake. It was a big stone house.

But we wasn't like the kids of today – you know, watching each other: 'Oh, you got that, you got that…' That wasn't even thought of. We was just brothers and sisters. Oh, our family life, it was beautiful. That's why I'm glad my daughter Nellie made up her mind to have Tanahya. (Although when she's older, she'll be saying to her, 'Where are you going?' and all of that, you know.) She's a beautiful kid.

Fair dinkum, I was a comical kid at school

I loved school but I was dumb. I never missed a day but I was as dumb as the dumbest. I suppose I loved just getting up to the school to play around. But the best thing I loved at the school was when we had cooking lessons. That's when we got older. That was lovely!

I went to school till I was seventeen. And I was only in grade five! It's just that I just loved school. I loved school but I didn't love learning. But I suppose I couldn't hook on to whatever was going on. Or I was just a lazy bastard – you know what I mean? I suppose I just didn't want to learn because I don't think I missed a day! I used to write my words out five hundred times. I used to have my best mate, Dorry Love (she's Dot Shaw now), I used to have her, and Turty (Myrtle Long [Kartinyeri]), and Ruth Campbell and that, doing all these pages of words. So that's the reason why I never probably learned them words. Yes – I was a good organiser... We was good mates...

I was at school with Mr Lawrie – but I don't think I was in his class. Henry was in his class, must have been. Oh, we had Mrs Lawrie. Well old Mr Lawrie – he went. That was the one who used to teach Mum and them. Then we used to have the other Mr Lawrie, and his old wife used to teach us; sitting down eating chocolates and teaching us.

That other Mr Lawrie – oh, he was a bastard. We used to have to take hankies to school every day. And me – always used to be in a hurry to go to school, so every day I used to rip my petticoat, and get a piece of rag off there. And I get a hiding from my Mum when I got home.

I was always rushing and I'd have my shoes on and my petticoat on. I used to get out of bed first thing in the morning and put my petticoat on, put my *gundies* on, put the coat on ('cause I loved my coat, 'cause my uncle got me my coat and it was so lovely). And I used to go straight to school with my little shoes on that my other old uncle, Uncle Banks got me. My mum's brothers used to help her with us kids. 'cause my dad used to work – he used to work hard but...

And one day it was hot and I went to take my coat off and I realised

I only had my petticoat on. Yeah. 'I've got to go home,' I said in a real sad way. 'I feel sick.'

So I went home and Mum said, 'Harriet!'

I said, 'I know. Look!' And I showed her.

She said, 'Youuuuuu!' And BANG! Hit me straight away.

So I put my dress on and put my coat back on and went straight back to school.

We used to line up to go into school. There was a Mrs Dabinett at school when I was there. I think she was Mrs Padman that lives here in Murray Bridge – an old family friend of hers. She used to come to school and learn us to cook and everything, you know. I loved cooking but if the teacher Mrs Dabinett and them started stirring the mixture, I'd just look at them, you know.

And they'd know that look, you know. And they'd say, 'Harriet, what's wrong?'

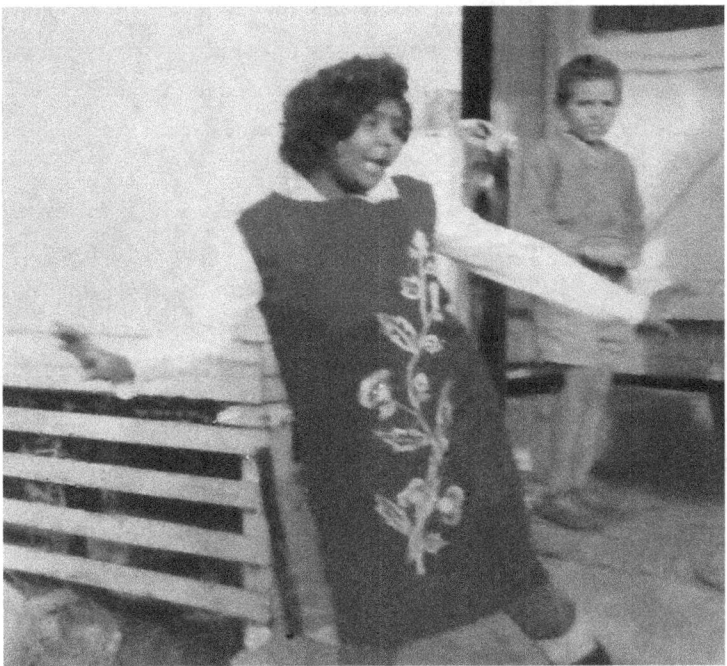

My sister Leah with Lawson Rigney outside the Rankines' residence! – our house at Raukkan. (Photo from the family's personal collection)

'How many times I got to tell you? If I'm mixing that now, it'll go back to what it was! It won't stay like that!'

They couldn't make me go up and mix that cake from the start to the finish because I was left-handed and they was right-handed. And I would not mix it. So I had to get sent back to the classroom. I wasn't a troublemaker. It was just that I had my own way with what I wanted to do.

We used to have one old teacher that used to smack us left-handers on the hands with the back of the ruler.

I said, 'You can flog me as much as you want over there with my left hand. But I'll never use my right hand!'

I wasn't learned that, I started with that! I was born with my left hand. But our old mother and father never ever smacked us or anything for using that hand. Some teachers used to flog us across the hands.

I used to say, 'I don't know why you're flogging me. Because you'll never change me.' I kept on going with my left hand. They couldn't stop me. 'You can flog me as much as you like but you won't learn me to use my right hand.' I was the only left-handed in my family.

Henry was left-handed when he was shooting. Nellie, my daughter, is left-handed.

In my mum's day – in her days – they was just brilliant writers! Wish I had the letter that my mum wrote. You should see her writing! And my sister Polly used to write like my mum, lovely writing. But Leah scribbled, Henry scribbles, I do, Sidney…

I started going to school when I was eight – eight or nine. So it must have been about 1952. But I don't think we started school early in them days. But everything that the teachers and that were saying to me – it sort of went straight through one ear and out the other.

Fair dinkum, I was a comical kid at school. And if I wanted to be nasty, I'd be nasty. All the kids and that, we got along all right. But if they hit me, I'd have a fight with them, no worries, you know. I had my brothers and that in school. I had brothers going to school with me – and I was just as good as them. With Henry and them, I was just as good at fighting; nobody would take me on. I was a horrible one – true! But I enjoyed my life at school.

That's how strict we was brought up

But I always think how lucky that we lived – 'cause my Mum had ten children and, you know, losing five of them. You know we had them as babies and we saw them and then they passed away. It sort of made us grow up, you know, in our ways. And my mum and dad used to argue like cats and dogs but that never used to worry us. Henry started working when he was about fourteen or fifteen in the dairy. Dad, he had been away, but when we was growing up, he was always there. Him and Henry always did the dairy together. I think Henry and Dad used to milk the cows – without the machines. Then we got the machines. I think before Dad went to the dairy, he was the butcher.

Him and Mum, they used to live at Block K. This was before we was born. Only my two sisters was living then, Polly and Leah. They used to have all these others – the Carter boys was with them. 'Cause we had another brother called George but I think he died before that. But they used to go Coorong and all. And the Carter boys used to go with them – like Dudley Carter and them. That's why we call them our

My father, Hendle Rankine, at the dairy at Glenora, just outside of Raukkan. (Photo courtesy of Dorothy French (Long))

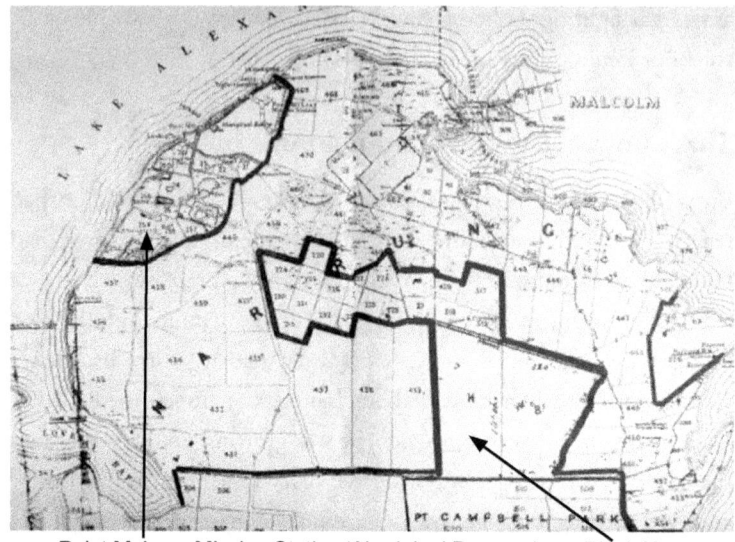

Point McLeay Mission Station 'Aboriginal Reserve'   Block K

Map of section of Lake Alexandrina showing Narrung area with Point McLeay settlement and hinterland, including Block K. (Map courtesy of Mrs Padman – given to her uncle, Narrung farmer settler, 1907)

grans: they Carters and we're Rankines. That's why I reckon we're so close now. From then onwards. Dudley Carter would be seventy-seven by now – or even older.

Down the Coorong, they'd be going fishing. My dad would go shooting – duck shooting. Like I say, we were brought up on ducks and rabbits and that. Then they got the butcher's shop. But Cecil Gollan was the butcher. Dad went from the butcher's shop to the dairy. He worked it for years and years. Then he got his horse and cart and he used to go rabbiting.

And Dad would go outside the house and throw a bit of bread into the Lake. And the silly old pelican would come down to grab it. And my dad would shoot it so my mum could make feather flowers. And that was another thing that bought money into the house. Our mum would sell the feather flowers to the Salvation Army. They came down the Lake on the steamer. But they were money-grabbing. They would only pay her two shillings and sixpence for a bunch. Later on, I could go into

My grandfather Henry Rankine with his daughter Auntie Nellie down on the lake. (Photo from the family's personal collection)

the museum in Adelaide, make feather flowers and get $36 a bunch!

I can only remember once seeing the steamer. When the steamer used to come along the Lake, we wasn't allowed to run along the Lake. We all lived along the Lake but we weren't allowed to just run down to it. We was only allowed to stand outside the house and watch it. That's how strict we was brought up.

We – like Dorry, me, Beryl, Ruth, Hazel, Dot – all of us used to be in the choir. And we used to go to Adelaide and sing at the Unley Town Hall. The Raukkan Choir – Peter Rigney and all of us was in it. Conda; he used to play the piano. But it was good. But I wasn't allowed to go – only once or twice. Mum and them were strict with us. No saying like today's kids, 'Well, see you later, Mum, we're going camping…' or 'We're going with this fellas…' or 'We're going with that fellas…'

That was out! It's so what-you-call-'em now! See, all my mates had babies before me. But this was a strict bringing up. And I never even worried about any boyfriend.

She was a very strong woman my mum, Annie Isobel Rankine MBE

My sister Leah was taken away when she was young. She had a nervous breakdown. She got frightened with the horse and the cart bolting there. She was standing there and they were all jumping around her. They took her into Adelaide, into the hospital. Then she went from there to that hospital near the sea, Estcourt House; she was there. Then they took her up to Colebrook, Colebrook Home. And they

My mum, Annie Isobel Rankine, showing her MBE medallion to her brother, Uncle Banks Long, at the Tailem Bend hospital.
(Photo from the family's personal collection)

wouldn't let my mum take her. She was old enough to go to school and everything.

But one day they took her home, down to Raukkan. My mum didn't know that they took her down there but she *nukkin*, she saw Leah. She just went over and she grabbed her. 'Come on daught.' Leah was pulling away and she said, 'You're my daughter. Come on.' And she just told Sister McKenzie, 'I'll tell you, if you come near my house, you'll get no legs 'cause I'll just chop them off with a big axe!'

And Sister McKenzie came down there with the big boss. He couldn't do nothing about it. She was a very strong woman, my mum. She got the MBE, that old girl – made a Member of the British Empire. Yes, Annie Isobel Rankine MBE. That's how the Welfare used to act like that.

Henry, my brother – he's the one that followed in Mum's footsteps. Mum was chairperson of the Raukkan Council. They were on it together for a while. Then Henry was chairperson. Henry got an Order of Australia medal. He's very proud of it, my big brother.

My mum used to talk about the old times. But like I tell Nellie, I wasn't a person who would sit down and listen. I used to be more interested in what Dad was doing. My dad was a long way older than my mum. I was Daddy's little girl, you know. I was terrible. But

Marriage certificate.

my mum, I loved her. She used to go to church; she was a Christian woman.

But Father used to be a devil in disguise. *Pyan pyan*, swear, swear, swear, swear. But we still loved him – with all our hearts, you know. My dad – I can't tell you what my dad used to say… He never really stayed all his life down there, Raukkan. When he was young, he got into trouble and went to McNally's – Magill, see, used to be. And when he was about fourteen, they sent him up north after that. He told us all about the north – where he used to work. He been up there for years: Port Pirie and Port Germein – worked in a butcher shop, I think. He was born in 1899 and he went up there when he was fourteen. When he went up there, he had a little hat on with a mirror. Because that was from McNally's going out to work.

At Raukkan, we used to go spotlighting with Dad. It was beautiful. We used to go in a horse and cart, spotlighting rabbits. He used to have a battery in his cart and the spotlight hooked onto it. We wasn't brought up like most of them kids on Raukkan – they didn't have what we had. But we never ever throwed it up; we was all the same. We wasn't higher than anybody else. Not like nowadays Raukkan. It's

Me and Sidney.
(Photo from the family's personal collection)

who's got the best house, who got this and who got that. We never ever did that. And we're still not doing it.

I had a good life. Sidney did too. See, we was brought up that if Sidney or me had an argument with anybody, that was my argument; nothing to do with them. See? And that's why a lot of people here – if you argue with the person, now, these days, you're arguing with the family. But it's not supposed to be like that. You know? Because them fellas, 'Hello, brother,' they call Henry, my brother. And yet they walk past us. You know? But that don't hurt me. Because if they don't want to talk to me, stiff shit, you know. I don't care. I've got a lot of friends. But now, not like the old days, you argue with the person, it's with the whole family.

At Raukkan, they used to be terrible for not talking to each other – argue. Our neighbours used to be my mum's worst enemy. They used to call my mum everything. But me and Polly and them used to always stand by our mum. Because we used to work in Adelaide, we used to come home for the weekend. They might talk to us but not to her.

When we used to walk past them, they'd sing out, 'Hello, you girls from Sussex Street. Hello, Polly. Hello, Tot.' And they wouldn't say hello to my mum and Leah.

I used to say, 'Oh Mum, just let me go and smash them!'

She used to tell us, 'No, that's not your argument. You just keep your hands to yourself. That's your family on your father's side. If they want to pick on me, they're not hurting me!'

Raukkan Church and part of the hall before its restoration. (Photo courtesy of Dorothy French (Long))

I said, 'I don't care.'

'No,' she said. 'You respect your elders.'

Oh, I used to get wild.

I reckon it was her old father that made her strong like that: Clarence Long, Milerum. That's who we all descended from, the Longs and the Rankines. He was gone, I think, before me and Sid was born. My mum used to talk about him. She used to say that he was a very proud person. He used to walk all around down the Coorong, *unna*?

That's why when we see George Trevorrow and them, because they're from the Coorong, we call them Coorong breed: 'Hello, Coorong!'

And they say, 'Hello, Coorong!' back.

We don't call each other by our names. That's because of Grandfather coming from that area, see.

There were eighteen groups in the Ngarrindjeris, Sid says. He knows because he does a lot of talking to a lot of people. Where I don't.

Grandfather Clarence Long, my mum's father, is on the $50 note standing in front of the church at Raukkan with his first wife. He was the last initiated Ngarrindjeri man. Von Doussa Long was my mother's brother. His son Persil (Gilbert Long, Dorothy's father) is me, Henry and Sid's first cousin. When my son Tony was born, I named him

Anthony Von Doussa Rankine because I loved my uncle's name so much.

We've got some things, family things. Susan is Henry's daughter. She's the oldest granddaughter, so therefore she's got some of the things like Mum's MBE. That's how our family worked it out. Nellie's the second-oldest granddaughter. She's got some things because she's good at keeping things and because Leah passed them on to her.

Going out to work

My sister Leah, her and Polly started working in Adelaide first. I wasn't allowed to – I was too young. I left school when I was about seventeen but I was working for the people what was the boss of Raukkan: like the manager and all that. It was all right – I enjoyed myself working for them. It was only about £17 or something. We used to iron, wash their clothes, iron their bloody clothes! They never had to do it for themselves. Never! That's what I said: I'll never ever do that for another white person – if anybody tell me to iron their clothes, I'll tell 'em where to go.

Polly and Leah went to work at Sussex Street first. It was an old church, a big old place it was, in Lower North Adelaide. It was for young people, and from the north they was coming – kids were sick and everything. Me and Sidney used to go down there for the weekends with Polly and Leah. We was home, Raukkan and Polly and Leah used to work Sussex Street.

And then Leah left Sussex Street and she used to work at another factory – spices or something. Then I got a job there when someone else left. This woman used to go to the north and bring back these kids. I can see her face as clear as crystal. Not Mrs Angus – she was for this end. They would say that we were bringing them down to go to the hospital and then they were gone… They were terrible in them days. (Even with our own cousins – like Margaret got taken away from her mum. And Jack, Alex and Larry, her brothers. That was Mum's sister, but she was home, Victor Harbor, Port Elliot, when they got taken away.)

And Polly used to work at Sussex Street – and then I started. And

Me and my son, Tony, at 52 Sussex Street, Lower North Adelaide. Leah brought him down from Raukkan to see me. (Photo from the family's personal collection)

then Leah had little Sidney and went home Raukkan. I was jumping here and there working for different white people in Adelaide. 'Cause I didn't like them people there, so I'd go back to Sussex Street. And they'd give me another place to go to work.

Yes, Sussex Street was for young people coming from the north. Kids were sick and everything. So Polly and Leah started working there 'cause there was other fellas working there before Polly and Leah. But we was there the longest.

It was excellent at Sussex Street. All the kids, the babies coming from the north, and we had to look after them and take them to hospital and all that. It used to be lovely. I enjoyed it. I think that's where we got our experience for looking after our own kids when we had them. We knew what to do. I enjoyed it down there. And all the old girls that used to chew tobacco – you know, the *pitjuri*. They used to go behind the shed.

And another thing that they used to do was 'Harriet! Have you got any clothes – old clothes?' So I used to give them all the clothes that

My grandfather
- my Mum's father,
Clarence Long *(Milerum)*.

(Map courtesy of Mrs Padman – given

1907 map of the Coorong and Environs showing Point McLeay (centre)

uncle, Narrung farmer settler, 1907)

Me on my twenty-first birthday at Raukkan. My sister-in-law Jean's brothers and sisters are looking on. 'I'm wearing my present – Ringo Starr's guitar.'
(Photo from the family's personal collection)

was in the cupboards and that. So they used to cut all them clothes up and make a quilt; sew the patchwork on to the blanket – grey blanket. Oh, they used to be clever. Me and Polly just used to sit down and watch them. Yes, we used to enjoy our life with them gang. That's why I never walk past any of them when they here in Murray Bridge.

That's how we was brought up: respect other people and they respect you. And even with white people, the same. You know, I could walk in the pub down here in Murray Bridge and sit down and play the pokies and that and I got all them fellas saying hello to me; that's black and white. And yet some fellas going in there and don't want to talk to anybody. But when you're home by yourself, you don't talk to nobody, *inna*? And as soon as you go out, you've got all these fellas there – have a good yarn! Yes, I've got a lot of time for a lot of people. Whereas they haven't.

I had another place where I used to work: down Unley Road, where

I used to do housework. And I used to have another little sleepout outside there. Just one room. Oh, it used to be beautiful – but I was frightened. I used to be that frightened. I'd never been sleeping in a place by myself. I was scared. They were new Australian fellows too, I think they were Italians. But they were beautiful. They had three daughters. They'd all get our names from Mrs Angus – she was working there in the office near Hindmarsh Square. We used to be home, Raukkan and then went to Sussex Street and then she got us a job.

Because we used to work in Adelaide, we used to come home for the weekend. Dorry Love (Dot Shaw she is now), she was my best friend on Raukkan; we used to work and she had to give her money to her mother and father. But I was allowed to keep mine so I used to shout her to the pictures. Dorry's got six or seven children now and I only got two. But every time I see her, I think how we never used to worry about boyfriends and that. But then she was married to Edward Love with Matthew and Ian and then she met Jimmy Shaw. Dot and Hazel took over working at Sussex Street – Hazel was her sister.

Up to Woomera

Well, I think that's when I went up to Woomera. I had a corker kid – looking after him: Kirk, Kirk McTaughlet. I wonder where he is now...

When we went to work up at Woomera, me and my sister Polly, we went to the People's Palace, used to be. We went there and we stayed there – and then we got a pass from the Aboriginals Department to go up on the train and go up to work at Woomera. No money in our pockets. We had written on the pass what we could have – a piece of paper so we could have a feed and then go on to Woomera.

Everyone had a passbook to come into Woomera. And we had our cousin Mal – Mal Sumner; him and Sister Sharkey used to live at that little place near Woomera – Pimba. And we had to show our passes to say that we were just going out there for half an hour or an hour, to meet our relations. It was beautiful because we had Nellie Buckskin and Violet Buckskin and a couple of other girls there that we ended up working at Sussex Street with. We met Nellie and them on the train when we was going up there, going up to Woomera.

We were there, Woomera, working for whitefellas cleaning their house in the days of pounds, shillings and pence. I can't remember how much we were getting. I was only about eighteen. Yes, there was a couple of other girls – from Point Pearce – that was up there already and besides there was me and my sister.

But we never used to talk to anybody. Not to white people if we was put on the train or that. We were brought up not to go gossiping. Not like now! My poor old dad or mum – they'd hit me fair across the ears if they see how I talk to everybody in Murray Bridge! In them days we weren't allowed to mix up with nobody – with the white people and even with Point Pearce fellas. Or Port Augusta. This was about 1960.

About twelve months we was there. We Nungas had to get a pass to go here and go there, *unna*, if we wanted work anywhere. My sister Polly had her son and he had to get a pass from the Welfare in Adelaide, from where Margaret was looking after him, to take him home, to go home to Point McLeay so Leah could look after him! It was horrible! And now – it's strict and all that but they letting us be ourselves! You know what I mean? I mean that's not very far back, *inna*, is it, when you think about it?

We used to go and sit at each other's place

At Woomera, that old girl, that *mimini*, what I was working for, she used to do their own ironing. The first time, I used to just clean the house out and look after their little son, Kirk. He was a corker little kid. Because they were both working for the Rocket Range out there. One was from Germany – her husband – and she was from New Zealand. Oh, that was all right. I enjoyed it up there. Yes, when you work for white people, you've got to respect them, *inna*? That's how we was brought up: respect other people and they respect you.

Yes, we might have went down only twice to see Cousin Mally and Sister Sharkey all the time we was there – it was too much bother! You had to go and sign all these things… See, Fran – Fran Lovegrove – his aunty used to work up there in Woomera at one of them places where they go and take photos. If you was coming away from up there, you had to go and report, and show them your photo if you was coming down for a holiday or something. And she wouldn't even talk to us! Probably because she didn't know me! She was making out she was a whitefella – because she was light and everything! Mavis was her name. She ended up over in America. It didn't worry me! I didn't care who wanted to act black, who wanted to act white. They act white – I don't care.

When I wasn't working, I'd go up and visit Polly. Polly and me, we used to go and sit at each other's place where we used to work. McTaughlet, that woman that I used to work for – that's what their name was. (That's good memory, *inna*?) Yes, we always stayed together, me and Polly. Polly went to work for somebody else with ten kids.

And when you'd go into that house, you'd see all the model aeroplanes that they used to do up. And the ceiling – you couldn't see the ceiling.

And I used to say to Polly, 'You don't have to dust all them, do you?'

And she said, 'Harriet! Knock it off talking stupid!'

And I said, 'Well, how do you get on with all them kids here?'

She said, 'Well, I just go down and get in my room.'

True as God, we only did one trip from up that way in a car. That was our last trip. Oh, true as God it was that long! I was glad when it started getting dark and that, 'cause I was just sleeping. We were taking a little joey down for my brother, Big Sid. We put the kangaroo in the box and put all sorts around him to keep him warm when we went down to town. We went down Leah's, at Brompton, in Adelaide, where her man was. When we got to town to Leah's, the little joey, the poor little bastard, was as stiff as a post!

And Leah's man, Ronnie, that she had living there – they were living there in the caravan at Brompton – he went and buried it. And Leah's dog, Terry – he was an Alsatian – dug it up and ate it! It must have been about 1963 and I must have been about twenty.

Anyway, I didn't even go with any *kornis*

Yes, we were there in Woomera a good twelve months, I reckon. We enjoyed ourselves. They used to have their open picture theatres. We used to go there. Violet Buckskin (that's Nellie Buckskin's sister), she came from Point Pearce. She married a German fella from up there, Woomera, too. But we only just met up with each other up there – and we only just found out that we was related. My aunty who I'm named after used to be really close friends with Nellie's mum.

'That's why,' Mum said, 'you fellas were so close, because you were relations.'

I think her mum's name was Bessie. The father's name was Les Buckskin. But I think they've passed away.

But no, I never even thought about going out like that, like Violet. And that's why my daughter Nellie never had a baby till she was in that older age group. That's why it makes me wild when I see teenage girls having babies, because their life is already finished. They got nothing. No enjoyment. Nothing. That's what makes me wild with these fellas – and their mothers.

'Oh, what a beautiful little baby!'

That's deadly, having a baby. But who's going to look after it? Yes, my mum was right bringing me up that way. But anyway, I didn't even go with any *kornis*, any men.

Then we left Woomera. Oh, it took forever to get down to Adelaide. Then we went out to Sussex Street. Polly got a job there again and I went home to Raukkan. Yes, we were homesick. We used to go home weekends from Sussex Street but when we were in Woomera – no way was I going back all that way!

I wasn't that old but I was brought up strict – me and my sisters. I still never even thought about going with mens.

I was working at Sussex Street again after that. I was on the table, scrubbing, and I said, 'I wish I could slip off this table and I wouldn't have to do any more scrubbing the walls.'

And I did! And I slipped! And I cracked my leg and I had to get up to the hospital. And that doctor, he was lifting my dress up above my knees.

And I said, 'No. Not any further than that.'

He said, 'I'm a doctor!'

I said, 'I don't care who you is!'

The police used to come in there every night!

Then we used to go to the pub – the Carrington Hotel. Oh, the police used to come in there every night! We used to go up there to play eight ball and that. Well, that was the start of it – eight ball. After that, we started to have a couple of drinks. I was in Adelaide working. Yes the police used to come every every night 'cause the police station was just close, but they never worried us – me and Polly and all the other Sussex Street gang. The police used to just come looking for fellas.

They all just gone now; passed away. But a lot of fellas are still here. Anna Kelly, she used to be there. That's my best friend. And Merlene Miller, that's another friend. Lorraine Kelly and Martha Guerkin. There used to be a lot of us. We was all family because we all worked together; they was all working at Sussex Street too. Val Power used to work there too, and Tiggy. We were all young then. We were all dopey drawers together. About seven or eight of us used to work there – but it was beautiful because we loved all them kids.

We was still at Sussex Street in Lower North Adelaide when they had them tents and all that near there. Yes, the Aboriginal Embassy was there in North Adelaide…

I met Tony and Nellie's father

I had Tony when I was twenty-seven and Nellie when I was twenty-eight. Going to my cousin's house in Norwood, that's where I met Tony and Nellie's father: a big, tall Western Australian young blackfella. He was about six foot something. He was the father of both my kids – I wouldn't even think of going with anybody else. That's what we was brought up

*Tony and Nellie at the Christmas tree at Raukkan.
(Photo from the family's personal collection)*

to – not going with this fella to that fella, from that man to that man. When you was brought up with what we was brought up with, you respect what you was brought up with. Well, that's how I think.

I was in Adelaide working and I had Tony. When I was about twelve or thirteen, one of my brothers hit the horse I was on and I fell off the horse the way I was sitting on it – fell on my knees. So my back somehow is curved; I think that's the word for it. With Tony being born, they said, 'Push! Push!' for twenty hours and then worked out what was wrong and I had a Caesarean. I had to go through that pain. I was glad that my son came first, and as soon as I took him home, I knew Leah would start saying, 'Oh, I'll mind him while you go back to work.'

My sister Leah looked after him and I went back working at Sussex Street, which was good. There was more money in there 'cause it was only £15 for endowment – not like now. And we used to send half our pay home to Leah 'cause she had Polly's son, Frederick – Fred – as well. And we went back and worked.

And then we got sick of work. I had Nellie at the Queen Victoria. With Nellie, they'd already worked out what was wrong, why I couldn't have natural birth, so they took me in and then I was out so quick. Then I went home Raukkan with my baby daughter. Yes, I went down to Raukkan and that's where I stayed; grew up Nellie and Tony down there. We were just up on the road there, the first house when you're coming in. My mother was passed away but my dad was there. Dot Shaw was there, and Beryl; they were my best friends.

Tony and Nellie's father, he went back home to WA. Rossie Jones was his name. He passed away. Marj – she used to be in Murray Bridge – she was his cousin. His daughter Jocelyn come over here and visited my kids. After thirteen years of phone calls!

Everybody knows us in Murray Bridge

We come up here, Murray Bridge, when Nellie was only six or seven. That's why everybody knows us. We wanted to move out of Raukkan. It was getting too boring on there. That's when I had the time of my life looking after my dad, here at Hill Street.

He wasn't really sick; he was just getting old. He was pretty good till right to the end. He never tried to run away or anything but just towards the end, he used to call me his sister's name, Joyce. 'Joycie! What you sitting there, just looking at me for?'

''Cause I'm frightened you just don't fall off that f— bed there!'

He said, 'I'm all right!'

I just used to sit there with him on the bed. I used to put him on the toilet and all, in that same room. No, no carers' money in them days. How many years did I look after him? Six or seven. Yes, in the last couple of weeks he'd call me Joycie or Ellie – after all his sisters.

I'd think, 'What's the matter with you, you dumb bastard.' I'd say, 'I'm your daughter – I'm Totty!'

'Ah, my girl. Come here!'

Yes, they were all saying not to take Dad away from Raukkan because he'd die. But look how long he lasted here four or five years! That's not my brother talking, but my relations, and they didn't know nothing. It's terrible my mother and father had so many children and lost so many. But it was beautiful. Never mind that my mum was going to church and my dad was a devil. But he was beautiful. I loved my dad. I would never have changed that relationship with me and my dad.

And when my dad passed away, who should pop in but Ivan Rigney. So I used to look after him! And he'd had a stroke and he was trying to say something, opening up his mouth… Then he'd wet his finger instead and draw on your hand one or two letters. He'd start off with a letter and then we'd have a guessing game about the word. But

Me in Murray Bridge.
(Photo from the family's personal collection)

he used to be deadly! He was brainy. He used to go to the races and come home rich! But still wouldn't give us anything.

He'd plant his tablets from us. Till I'd found his plant and I'd say, 'I found the place where your tablets is!'

And he'd say, 'No, no, no!' (He could say that: 'No, no, no!')

He stayed with us for a while, a long time. I think he went to hospital, then Elizabeth – Lizzie Rigney – started looking after him; that's her brother, her eldest brother. I'm glad Lizzie took over. I'm not going to look after anybody else. They have to look after me now!

From Hill Street, Nellie and Tony used to walk up to school – primary and then high school. Nellie used to get scared. She thought she was going to get taken away. She probably used to eavesdrop and heard us talking about the murderers – about the body that was found

Tony and Nellie going to school. (Photo from the family's personal collection)

in the Port River in the bag, cut up. She used to be real frightened – always thought that something was going to happen to her and Tony. My sister Polly used to call them 'Western Australian bastards!'

We were in Hill Street there – that house there straight across from the fire station. We saw that built. And we saw Graham, the electrician that goes around here fixing lights and that, we saw him mucking around with the hose, turning the tap on so the water would go all over the place – this way and that way. Because he was a little skinny fella, *unna*? We just used to sit outside and laugh and laugh and laugh, you know.

Oh, they used to run when the fire used to be somewhere in Murray Bridge. We used to hear that thing go. We used to shoot outside and watch that. And they'd get on their little outfits, running and jumping on the bus, the fire engine.

And I'd be saying, 'I hope they don't miss that bus!' Because we'd all be crying with laughter and we wouldn't be able to go and help them, you know.

And the driver used to look in the glass and he'd just steady down so they could get in.

That was lovely that old Hill Street house but we had the next-door neighbour on that side, the old cow.

'Oh, I'm just sick of your children throwing fruit in my yard!'

I said, 'Couldn't you see the limb hanging over that way, you dumb old…? The apricots off the tree is falling in your yard. It's not the kids throwing it in there.'

Oh, we used to have arguments but we didn't move to Mulgundawah Road just because of her. Leah was living in McHenry Street. She might have been a small little woman but no one could put it over her. Later on when Nellie got nervous and couldn't leave the house for two and a half years – yes, two and a half years! – she finally left where we were living later on in Standen Street and walked around to Leah's.

You can see from the photo how glad her aunty was – that Nellie had finally got out. After two and a half years!

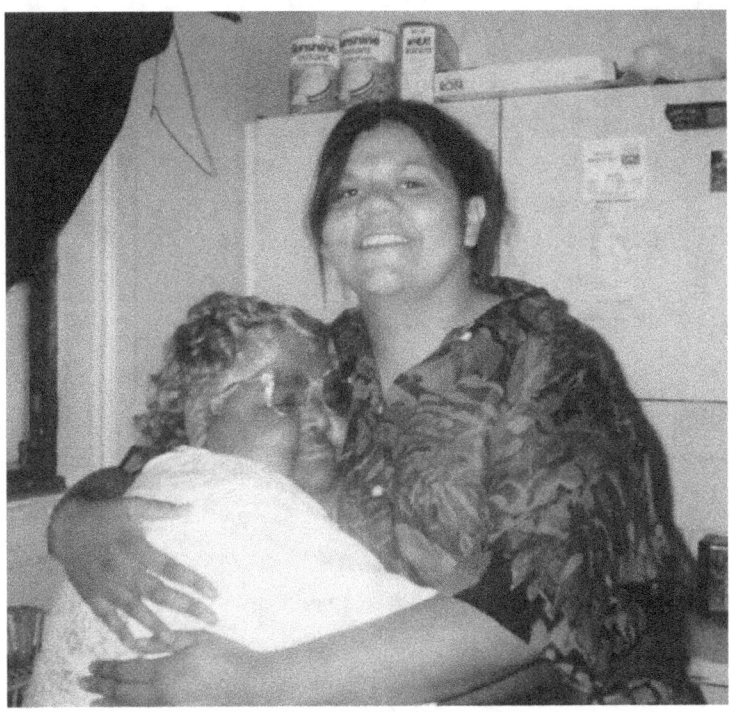

(Photo from the family's personal collection)

And in all that time, you know who stayed with her – who stayed with her in the house? Me! Her old mum. And I'm still with her! Her and Tanayha.

(From Nellie: That's unconditional love for you. That's real unconditional love!)

Epilogue

While I was writing my book, my only son passed away – the apple of my eye. Course he was! He and his wife Stella, they gave me my first two grandchildren, Leah Cheree and Anthony Von Doussa. And Nellie and Darrin Scott (Slippery) Wilson gave me my third grandchild Tanayha. Corker!

No one quite like you

A person that's considered One of a kind,
Is a person that's so hard to find.
The person gives you life, the will to survive,
The motivation to go on through the journey of time
This person is never the same as anyone else,
Her heart is always an open house.
Seeing me stumble, seeing me fall,
Praising me up as I learn how to crawl.
She'll come to painful tears,
As she witnesses my young fears.
But she'll never turn away from me,
That I earnestly believe.
So soft and so dear,
You helped me out when I kept you here.
As You play'd the bigger part, (MUM)
Every beat of my achin' heart.
Without the love you showed me,
Darkness is all I'd be able to see.
You're one amazing lady, that You know,
But once again, You need to be told.
Strength You gave, it helped me through this,
Felt like the answer to a young man's wish
That's why 'No-one's Quite Like You'
So thankyou Mum for helping me through!!
Harriet Agnes Rankine, words do express a lot.
These are just a few,
I have more to say as I love you, my dearest old Mumsy.
    Anthony xxx 5/1/2000

Word list

Ngarrindjeri	English
gundies	bloomers
inna? / unna?	isn't it? / wasn't it?
korni(s)	man, men
mimini(s)	woman, women
ngaitji	friend/totem
nukkin	look, see, saw, see you
pyan	swear/swearing
thukari	bony bream (fish)
pitjuri (Pitjantjatjara word)	bush tobacco
Nungas	general word for Aboriginal people in southern SA

Me, Leah and Nellie next to Nellie's beautiful painting at Murray Bridge South School. (Photo from the family's personal collection)

Outback Heart

Audrey Wonga
(Antikirinya/Yankunytjatjara)

Dedicated to my kids and my grandkids and to all my future grannies that I might one day have but I won't be round to see them.
And to all my next, next, next generations,
and to all my close relations:
Hele and Dodd families
Amos family
Bailes family
Stewart family
Aitken family
Finn family
Lennon family
Klembt family
Jones family
Woodforde family
McCallum family
Walker family.
Hope I didn't forget anyone.

Palya! Ngayuku tjukurpa, from little girl right up to *kuwari,* now. *Ngayuku* family will read 'em. 'Oh,' and *ngayuku puliri tjuta* and *pakali tjuta* will read it, 'Oh, *palya!*'

It's good to have made my book. This is my story from a little girl right up to now. My family, including my granddaughters and grandsons, will read it and 'Oh, that's good!'

Audrey Wonga, Umoona Community Coober Pedy,
13 October 2009

Taken away to Colebrook

Well, I was taken away at Anna Creek Station when I was a baby – 1958 – 'cause I had an abscess under my left armpit. And my mother was only fourteen. They took me in the Flying Doctor's and then Mr Weightman, he told my mother I wouldn't be going back to her because she was only fourteen when she had me on 17 October 1958.

I can remember years ago when I was small, I was at Colebrook Home in the Adelaide Hills. Mr and Mrs Francis were there. Every afternoon, she'd dress me up in this old-fashioned clothes and I had a big basket of flowers – and Mr Frances would paint me. It was a big portrait! I don't know where it is now. I'd love to see that before I die. I don't know where it would be.

I can just remember Maureen Marks, 'cause Maureen used to look after me. Then I found out Maureen was my aunty. I think Margie Crompton knew me from Colebrook. When I was a baby, I remember a big gum tree and a rope swing and the other kids always used to like pushing me. And one day they pushed me too high and I got scared and screamed out and Mr Francis comes out and grabbed all the kids.

I remember on Saturday mornings when it was cold, we used to all get dressed in our winter clothes, have proper gumboots. There was one big oval there. We used to go out and look for mushrooms. And they were real big ones too! Not like button mushrooms – these were really big ones! Pick them and then go back and then we'd have mushroom and gravy on toast for breakfast.

I can't remember going out from there – I just remember all the good things. I remember one night, I don't know whether it was true, we was all sitting out on the veranda, we seen the face in the moon. I was too young but someone must have tricked me somehow but I always remember these two eyes. Someone must have tricked me somehow but I seen it myself. They might have put funny glasses on me and said, 'Look at the moon.'

Colebrook had a reunion a couple of years ago – 2007 – and I was supposed to go but the plane ticket mucked up. And I cried too when I came back from the airport here in Coober Pedy. I bought myself a couple of beers and I sat down and cried! And Nola Boland who was organising it for me, she came and sat down with me and cried too! I went out to the airport and they had misplaced my ticket.

And on the way back to town, they rang to say, 'They've found your ticket. You can go back now.'

And I said, 'No, I feel too thing now…'

Plaque at the site of Colebrook Home.
(Photo courtesy of Mary Pullen)

Nola said she could organise for me to go down there and I could take my daughter with me. That'd be even better. They had a plaque too made, of all the kids who lived in Colebrook – put their names on there. Mine's on there, not as Wonga; when I was small I was known as Audrey Anderson, my mother's maiden name.

There's one woman I was talking to on the phone, she said, 'Oh, who are you?'

And I said, 'Audrey.'

'Oh, Audrey, your name's on the plaque too!'

Yes, I'm sure that was Avis. She runs a hostel on Payneham Road in Adelaide. That's where I was going to stop with her.

At Sussex Street

I remember when I was small, I think I was at one home in North Adelaide – I think it was Sussex Street – my mother used to come down. There was one old lady there and my mother and that old lady used to take my sister and me for a walk to the park – just across from the river there. And maybe charging on and talking language, drinking. That's why I kept my language, I think.

I think I was about six or seven. My mother was always bringing my sister down to see me.

I remember one day me and my sister Marlene was in this room, we found this real flash handbag. We thought it was a toy but when we opened it, there was a purse in there with money. And we said, 'Oh, look here – money!' We don't know about stealing then. Grabbed some money and we ran off to the shop then. It was one of the worker's purse. We kept saying, 'No, we never touched it.'

They interviewed us and they put something in front of us to play with and they got our fingerprints off that!

See, my mother couldn't talk English properly and she'd talk language to me, and my sister would laugh at me first and I'd just look at her.

'What did she say? Tell me what she's saying.'

Marlene would turn around then and tell me then in English. Then she'd tell me in language things – tree, *punu*, birds, *tjulpu* – and all that. And every time they used to come down, I'd remember them words. And then when my mother used to talk with me in language, I'd understand her.

Coober Pedy

The Welfare would take me up to Coober Pedy when my mother was there – on the bus with a Welfare official. They'd leave me there for a while. On the Reserve at Umoona there was a big house where Colleen Tschuna used to stay. I used to stay with her. My family could come and visit me then. Mum (Gloria Anderson) and the family were living on the flats where those little tin houses were in on the Reserve where the toilets are now. They were in one of the isolated ones separate from the others. I was a bit shy at first but then I got used to it. Later on, the Welfare would come back up on the bus and pick me up again to take me back to Adelaide.

The only original house on the Reserve that's still standing is old *Tjilpi* Marousen, *inti* – old Man Marousen's, isn't it? It's a one-bedroom tin shack. And they had an old wagon there too out the front but they took it to the Umoona Opal Mine Museum. (Yanni is only leasing that from Umoona Council. Some of the profits go to schooling for our kids to go to boarding school at Rostrevor in Adelaide.)

Umoona Reserve (now Umoona Community), established in 1959 with Pastor Fred Traeger as the administrator. These tin houses were demolished in 1999. (Photo courtesy of the Traeger family)

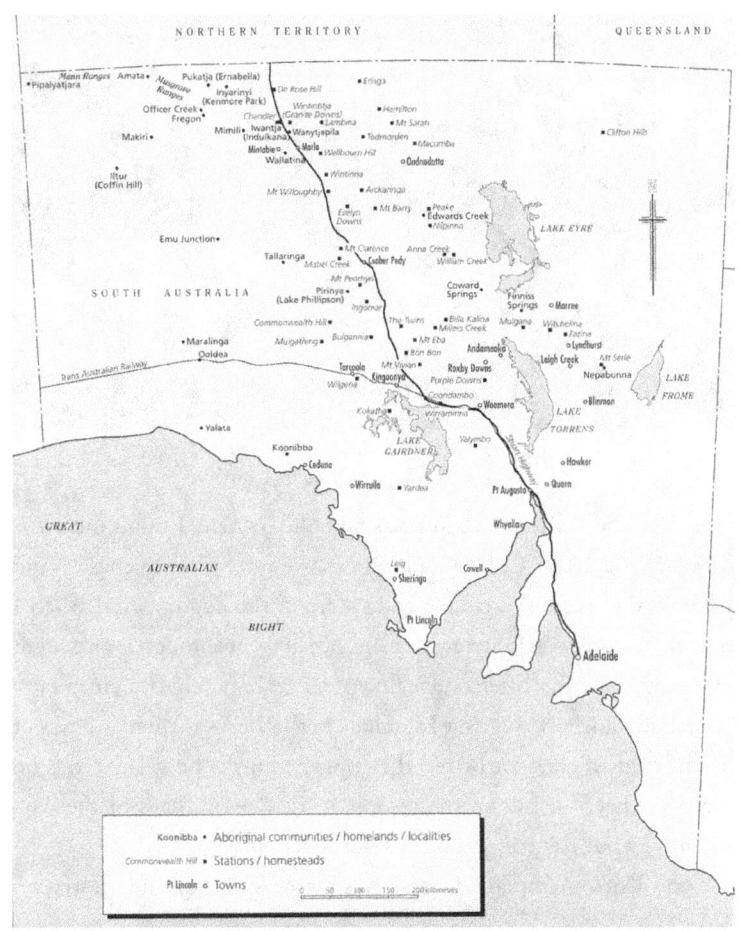

North and west of South Australia.
(Map courtesy of Umoona Community Council, Coober Pedy)

to school. There was a man called Ivan *kungka palya*. He was real good to us. Sometimes he'd take my parents out noodling – out for opal. And he'd leave them out there. And at dinner time, he'd meet us at the gate with lunch – he'd have fruit for us. He was real good to us, the ones he knew properly, but he used to be an old larrikin man so they said. That's what he was always saying to the *kungkas* – to the A*na*ngu women: '*Kungka palya*, nice woman.' That's the way he got the name. That's what all the A*na*ngu used to call him.

At the reserve there – at the house they used to call the 'Little

*L to R: my mother Gloria, Patricia and Kathy.
(Photo courtesy of Kathy Wonga))*

House on the Prairie' – when I was on holidays here, I think there was Monkey and *Tjilpi* Carroll and Kingey, we were playing chasie. And I was in the dugout, a couple of us were in the dugout. And when I ran out, I tripped, tripped my leg up. A nail went through it and it got infected. I was about ten. I got flown out to Port Augusta Hospital – it was the old Port Augusta Hospital. My father was there – he'd got burnt. And when I got better, they put me on the bus. There was no room so they put me on the middle to sit down. That's in the days when they put passengers on the floor too.

And Uncle Aeroplane George was there. And they said, 'Sorry, no room.'

And I said to him, 'Where're you going?'

And he said to me, 'Oh, I'll see you in Coober Pedy – see you tomorrow.'

When the bus come in, in Coober Pedy, we pull up – I think it was where the old Breakaways Café is now, there was a *kungka* there. I forget her name.

She said, 'Oh you come back? You want an ice cream?' So she give me an ice cream.

And when I looked, he was sitting across the road smiling at me – Aeroplane George. They reckon he could travel around real quick. That's why we all knew him as Aeroplane George.

'Cause later on, when the Woma Centre was in town behind the Coober Pedy Council office there, me and Mindi Crombie was working there. And we always used to ask him, 'Eh, how you fly around?'

And he used to tell us to shut up and mind our own business. 'What are you asking questions for?'

Visiting in Coober Pedy to my family, that's how I got to go to school in Coober Pedy and you know how my cousin, Mindi Crombie, sings about the school in his 'Coober Pedy' song. He sings how we used to line up and march into school – well, that's true! And Kumana they called him – I can't remember his English name – he used to play the drums, he'd be the drummer boy. Yes, he'd be the drummer boy and we'd all march in, one, two, three, march into the classroom! All us *Anangus*, Aboriginal, kids with just a few white kids.

We'd have our showers at the Reserve there. Us kids had to be at the shower block early. We always used to have our own breakfast at home before that. There was a big truck, and Mindi's big sister Enid and her boyfriend Lionel Brown, they sort of was our elders.

And Mr Brown, Nita Brown's husband, he was in charge of the Reserve, he would come out: 'Enid, are all your girls here?'

And she'd look around and see. 'Yes, Mr Brown, they're all here!'

'Lionel, are your kids here?'

He'd count around. 'Oh, so and so's missing.'

'Oh, I'll catch him up in a minute.' And he'd tell the truck driver to take us to school!

It was a big truck and we'd all sit in the back.

My grandmother, Cockie's mother (Marlene Warren's mother), Rita Warren, and my *katja*, my son, Roy Warren, took us out for a holiday for a little while out to Ingomar. There was me, Cockie and Gingerlee and Arnold, their young *malyn*, young brother, we used to go to school with some other kids.

And then, if you was good, the teacher would take you first one on the motorbike to the tank to go swimming and you'd have the tank for yourself. If you was good and you was the first kid, and Gingerlee wasn't, Gingerlee would be there waiting and would give us a hiding over that.

Sometimes we'd get scared and say, 'No, I don't want to go first. Let him go! Let him go!'

And the teacher would say, 'But he hasn't been good today. You did good work today.'

'No, he can do it! He can do it!'

And I can remember, we went out shooting one day and we went over this sandhill and there was a big claypan down the bottom and – this is always in my head – and there was the biggest mob of kangaroo, led by one big white buck! At Ingomar Station. It was like they all got together in that one claypan.

I can remember going out for *mangatas*, quondongs. When we was here, Coober Pedy, we used to go out with Uncle Marty (Dodd) and Kangku_r_u Rita – went noodling. She had that little one, Robbie; we used to look after him while she went noodling and sometimes we had a crowbar and we used to carry Robbie around, me and Glenys, his big sister, and we'd dig for our own opals out on the cuts. Uncle Marty used to take all the kids out who could ever fit on.

Noodling on the dumps. L to R: Joan Russell, Jane Russell, Rita Dodd, Rosie Dodd, Sheila Gibbs. (Photo courtesy of the Catholic Church, Coober Pedy)

Before we jump on, we'd fill the car up with rocks. When you see bottles or tin or that, you'd grab a rock and see who could first hit it. That was our little game. For when we were travelling. We'd say, 'Bottle coming up! Tin coming up!' And see who could hit it first.

Being fostered

Later on, the Welfare officer would come again and take me back on the bus to Adelaide again. I didn't really like all the changing around. I didn't like Adelaide much. Even when I go down there now, I still don't like it.

In Adelaide, I shifted round to a lot of homes, foster homes, white people. I didn't like being shifted round much. I remember another home I went to, sometimes they'd take me to this place like a hospital and they'd put glue in my hair. With wires. I was thinking they were using me as a monkey! I don't know what it was. I think other kids too they did it to. Probably to see if we were brainy! Some people in the homes, they used to call us outside. 'Have you done a *kuna* every day?' If you haven't done a *kuna*, then they'd give us suppositories. I just think now the stupid little things they used to do: wire on your head; if you haven't done a *kuna* for the day, you'd have to have a suppository! So sometimes us kids we'd say, 'We've done it! Done it!'

I finished third year high school. Then my foster family moved down to Port Adelaide and I didn't want to really stop there. Because I was doing high school at Kapunda. And my foster-parents, they were Aboriginal – Aunty Norah Lindsay, that's my foster-mother. So I think Welfare found me a job.

The other day 2009, my cousin, Rameth Thomas, Aunty Colleen's son, was passing through. Aunty Colleen is my mother's sister. He's always passing through here, Coober Pedy. When I seen him, I pulled up next to him and I got out of the car and I said, 'Hey, Broth, how are you going?'

And while I was talking to him, there was another bloke in the car and out of the corner of my ears I could hear my niece talking to the bloke in the car, and asking him his name, and he said, 'Tony Lindsay.'

When I heard that, I rushed around to the car. 'How're you going, Tony? You know me?'

He said, 'Na-ah.'

I said, 'It's me, Audrey!'

Oh, he got really happy and he got out and we hugged one another. He said, 'I've always asked for you.' But he asked Rameth, 'Do you know Audrey Anderson?' and Rameth only knows me as Audrey Wonga or Hull!

So next trip that Rameth comes up, he'll probably bring Tony up again. I'd like Tony, my foster-brother, to meet all my kids and my grandkids. Yes, Tony's got kids and grandkids.

Working girl

So after I left the Lindsays, that was when I went back to Adelaide. I went working then. I worked at a lolly factory – I can't remember the name – and then I worked at a fruit factory, John's Fruit Factory. I was living at a girls home – the girls were young and working. I know it wasn't Tandara. Then I think Welfare found me a job – a live-in job with Mona Tur. I was her live-in nanny. She was at work at the university. So I had her two little ones, Renee and Simone. Take them to school, go home, clean up, do washing. Afternoons I had off so I'd watch TV or go for a walk. Go and pick the girls up, bring them home.

Catching the Ghan back home to family

My mother and I kept in contact and one day I earned enough money, I saved up a little bit and I told Joe and Mona, 'I might catch the Ghan back home, eh?'

She took me in and I caught the Ghan and got off the Ghan. My parents were at Todmorden Station then. And I stayed in Oodnadatta for a while.

When I got off the train, my grandfather, Old Paddy Mack – he was a big man – he came running up holding his trousers up. 'Huhh, huhh,' he was puffing, 'are you Kulani's daughter?'

I said, 'Ye...s.'

'Come with me. I'm your grandfather.'

And I thought he might take me to a nice house. He took me to a humpy! I camped in the humpy for a couple of days and my father, Ross Wonga, came in from the station – Todmorden Station – to pick me up. We had a shed up there in Todmorden. It was done up nice – my mother was a clean woman. When it was hot, sometimes she'd make a humpy outside there and we'd camp in the humpy. She'd have a double-bed mattress and a single bed in the humpy with a big windbreak and a fire, and my father would camp on the ground. And my sisters and my brother used to camp on the bed. 'Cause every morning she used to shake my father's blankets and they'd be centipedes everywhere.

I loved it at Todmorden. The boss used to get us to do odd jobs for him. And he let me do odd jobs in the homestead like clean the single men's quarters or help Mum with the washing and things.

And Marlene when she started getting a big girl, he said, 'Oh, come on. You can start riding horses now.'

My father and I went down to the yard there and Marlene was

L to R: Julie Amos, Mona Stewart, Janet Amos and Audrey Wonga at Oodnadatta. (Photo courtesy of Janet Amos)

sitting on this horse and she had the rein pulled one side and the horse was going round and round, 'Daddy, Daddy, get me off. Get me off!'

She's at Oodnadatta now, my sister, Marlene Wonga. But in those days, she kept riding and I was in town, back in Oodnadatta – I think I was a teacher's aide then and I remember her and Christine Jones, they came in there for a holiday. And they said, 'Come on, let's go on the train.'

And I said, 'Where we going?'

'Oh, we'll go to Coober Pedy for the races.'

So we caught the train down to Port Augusta and did some shopping. Caught the bus up to Coober Pedy then. We had the money then – we were all working. Single. I think there was only a couple of whitefellas on that bus and when a good song comes on the radio, us three, we were singing top note! We loved it.

It was still the old road and at Kingoonya we were saying, 'Shall we act like white people and have a beer?'

And we said, 'No. We'll wait for Coober Pedy. Save our money for there.'

Later life

From Todmorden, I went back into town – to Oodnadatta and I was working there at the school. I applied for the teacher's aide job and got it. It was just good, earning my own money. They got books there at the Oodnadatta about the school and that – my name's in the books. I enjoyed it – it was good.

And some of the kids now – they're big grown-up women and men now, and they still talk about me, you know. Pauline Lewis (Parrot, she was) when we are with friends now, she says, 'You know what? Audrey was my role model when I was small, I used to look up at her. And I always thought, one day, I'm going to be like her.'

I think that was because I was just going in there and getting jobs, being the first Aboriginal woman to get a licence and all that.

Well, after I was in Oodnadatta, I shifted out to Indulkana. I applied for a transfer to Indulkana. It was good living at Indulkana working there as a teacher's aide. It was good. I had strong connections there. Angelina Wonga from Indulkana used to live with my father. And then he met my mother. So he had two wives – at the same time. She's got a big son, Robert. But he passed away. Her son Frankie, Frankie's father is a white man. But there was all that strong connection. Then she had another son, David, from old Kenny Mick. And Angelina always classes my father as her husband. That's why I went to Indulkana.

And I met Jason's father there. Not met, I was sort of promised. It wasn't falling in love; but I ended up loving him. When Jason was small, I left him. I left him and went down to Port Augusta. And I went to do my enrolled nurse's training. I passed and then I found out I was pregnant, so I couldn't go in the hospital to work. I was pregnant with Alinta then.

And I always liked that name Alinta because I seen that picture, *Women of the Sun* and part one was about a girl named Alinta; a good little love story. It was on Austar lately. I loved that name. I always kept in my mind till I had a girl. So I got my Alinta. Jason was seven years old before I had Alinta.

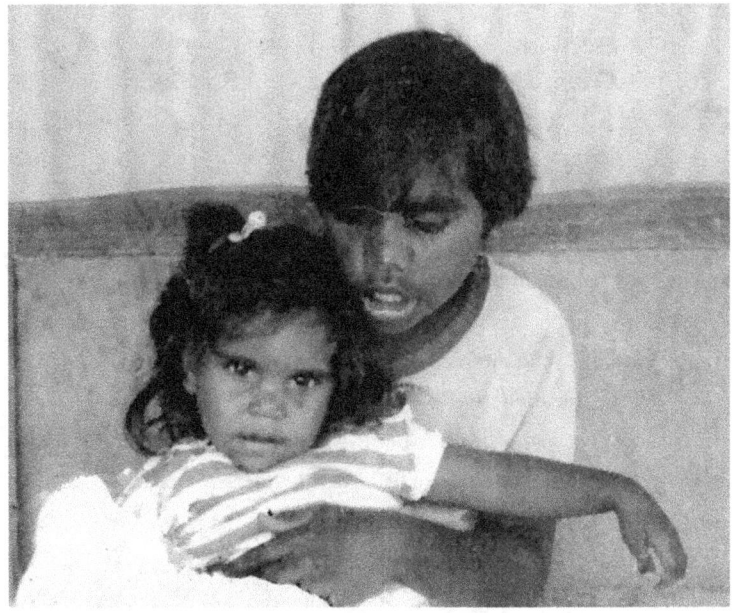

Alinta and Jason. (Photo courtesy of Serena Amos)

I was working down there – Port Augusta – working at the high school again. I married a Hull, Adrian Hull – that's how I got my Hull name – but people here in Coober Pedy still call me Wonga. I was there for years. But probably finding myself…and got into the drink. Realised it wasn't for me so I went back – to Oodnadatta. Those days in Port Augusta, I was a bit mixed up about how I'd been brought up. Just drinking… But no, the drinking didn't help.

When Alinta was small, about three, I was drinking every day and taking Alinta home with me. Colleen Warren, my aunty, heard about my drinking so she took Alinta home to live with her. I let her because I knew Alinta would be safe with her. Jason was with me. Jason was about ten.

When I used to go around to Aunty Colleen's to see Alinta, she wouldn't open the screen door. She'd always ask me, 'Are you sober?'

And I said, 'Yeah.'

'Let me smell your breath.'

And I went, 'Haah…' Then I was allowed to visit.

And after a while when I was ready to go, I got Alinta back. 'I'm going back to Oodnadatta – I've come to pick my daughter up.'

And we went back to Oodnadatta; A<u>n</u>angu call it Dunjibar. It was all right in Oodnadatta. I had family and I met Ronnie Lennon. I had three boys with Ronnie Lennon from there: Benji first, Ronald, and Ray. Ronald, he's named after his father, Ronnie. And Ray's named after his uncle, Ray Lennon, Sonya Crombie (née Lennon's) father. But I named Benji that because I always used to go down to Port Augusta to have my babies and Benji my brother always used to beg me, really sorry way – 'Sis, if you have a boy, will you please name it after me – please!' So I'd give in and say – 'Ye-ess – if it's a boy.' So he's Benjamin Ross – Ross after my father.

And after that my brother Benji – Benji Lennon – always used to come to Oodnadatta and tease little Benji and say, 'Heh, boy, who are you?'

And he'd look up and say, 'I'm you! Who are you?'

That was their little joke between themselves.

Benji. (Photo courtesy of Michele Madigan)

And he always said, 'You know I'm sick. I've got a heart problem.' (He had a hole in the heart.) 'If anything happens to me, don't call him Kumana – keep calling him Benji.'

My brother Benji was Lennon because Uncle Barney Lennon grew him up. What happened was my father and mother were drunk one night and Uncle Barney and Aunty Dorothy went shopping here in Coober Pedy, late afternoon, just barely evening. As they were going into the shop, they could hear this little baby crying and apparently the mother had left him behind the rubbish bin and took off. Must have forgotten him. So they picked him up and they seen his face and they said, 'This is my sister's kid. Well, I'm taking him home now.'

And Uncle Barney always said, 'That's what God gave us. That's our prodigal son. Because he was lost and then he was found! God gave us him.'

His name was Colin Lennon really. But he got the name Benji. He was really a Wonga. He was my mother and father's child. I never grew up with him but he knew who we were.

Wangka kulini

Last night me and my father (my father's brother) A<u>n</u>angu way were talking about the special language – the ceremony language… I know some words of it. He told me, 'Yes, that's how you say it.' I know a little bit because Frankie Wonga was out bush and I helped him. I had to stay up all night. That's because like I said, Angelina Wonga, his

Uncle Barney's daughter, Emsie, with her daughter, Denise, little Nellie and Audrey. (Photo courtesy of Kathy Wonga)

mother, used to live with my father. So I'm Frankie's big sister. Yes, I learned culture from her. I always take things around to her now she's old at Umoona in Aged Care.

And you know how I said I couldn't understand the language properly when I was small – well, my kids, they can understand it.

They won't talk it often unless we go somewhere where they don't want people to understand – then they'll start talking the language then. But it's good they can talk it! Yes, I've always told my kids, 'Heh, you've got to learn to talk the language and teach your kids to keep it so it goes strong.'

See, in New South Wales and even Adelaide or the Ngarrindjeri people, they can't talk their language. They might say a few words and then they've got to put the English word in it. Whereas we can speak our language and only use an English word that hasn't got a language word. Like 'toaster' or 'photocopier'.

Son Benji knows how to fish in the dams and all that there. 'Nana Kulani, Uncle Michael and Mum used to take us fishing, digging up frogs from the sand, track lizards down, perenties, goannas, and I know how to cook them,' says Benji.

L to R: Cheryl Stewart, Gail Margaret (peeping), Jason and Audrey.
(Audrey Wonga private collection)

Yes, all my sons are good hunters.

Wangka kulini. And they know language. They can speak to you in language.

Yes, I'm a grandmother

Yes, I've got grandchildren. First time you're a grandmother, you're really proud. Really excited and can't stop skiting. Everyone's looking, 'Oh, you're a grandmother, you're a grandmother!'

So then you get three or four, it's 'Yes, I'm a grandmother, I'm a grandmother again.' Like you're used to it. And you start ageing then! You realise.

Jason's got a big daughter, Leeanne. Jason's my eldest son. He's single. Jason's got three: Leeanne, little Kimberley passed away and then there's one little boy in Oodnadatta… Jason's little sly one. I call the little boy *tjamu*, grandson.

Alinta's with Andrew Dodd. She's got three boys now. I call them all my *tjamu* or *pakali*, grandsons. Alinta's kids, when you speak language to them, they understand. I like it sometimes when there's some words they're saying, like when they get on the couch chair and try to jump over and, '*Wa̱rarakati, wa̱rarakati*!' They love that word. And they kill themselves laughing. They think it's a funny word but they know what it means – 'Get off, get off!' But they speak English mainly but they understand what I'm saying. I always tell Alinta too, 'You got to talk language to them.'

Waltjapiti, family

You know, A̱nangu have got certain rules about family.

What happens is that you've got your father and mother and then your father's brothers, you call them *Mama*, Dad, and you call your fathers' sisters *Ku̱ntili*, Aunty. And your mother's sisters, you call them *Ngunytju*, Mummy, and your mother's brothers you've got to call them *Kamu̱ru*, Uncle. You can't call them Dad. You know where you stand when you call them 'Daddy, Mummy...' And your mother's sister's kids – whitefella way all first cousins – we call brothers and sisters.

Then you've got your grandparents: grandmother, grandfather; your grandkids – and your cousins – they're in one group. And your uncles and aunties, nieces and nephews they're in another group – *inyurpa*, we call 'em. So you know how they marry. They can marry *inyurpas*. It draws a line among who can live together. You've got two different groups of people.

But we can't marry that group. My *inyurpas* are uncles, aunties, nieces and nephews. But there's always one lot in the middle. The two outside lots (generations) can get together and marry and the other lot in the middle they can't. It's hard to explain but it's a good way. But some people break the rules. In the old days when people broke the rules, they'd get hunted away from their community and...

Back in Coober Pedy

I moved to Coober Pedy about five and a half years ago 'cause Alinta was having my grandson, Kyren. I stayed here for my grandkids. She had two more boys – she's got three altogether. I had a house way over

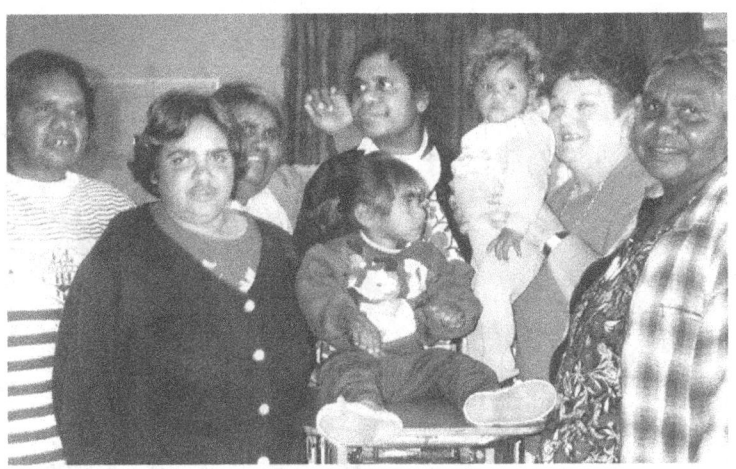

Back L to R: Marlene, Gloria, Kathy, Tammy and nurse.
Front L to R: Margaret, Tahnee and Millie Myson.
(Photo courtesy of Kathy Wonga)

Back L to R: Yuntu Spider, Janet Amos, Casey Helms, Peter Amos.
Front L to R: Samantha Amos, Carmen Amos, Serena Amos and Lorraine Jones.
(Photo courtesy of Janet Amos)

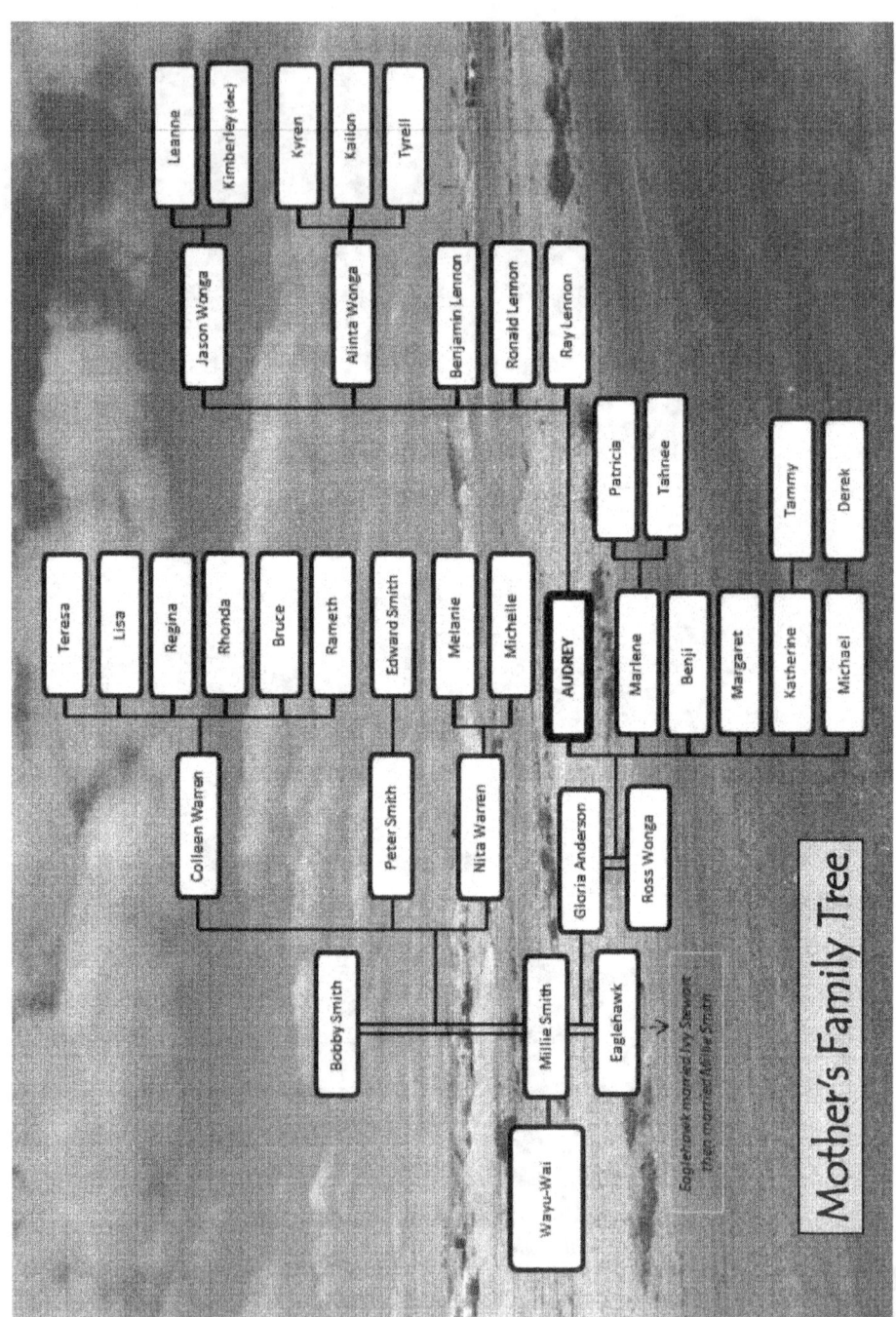

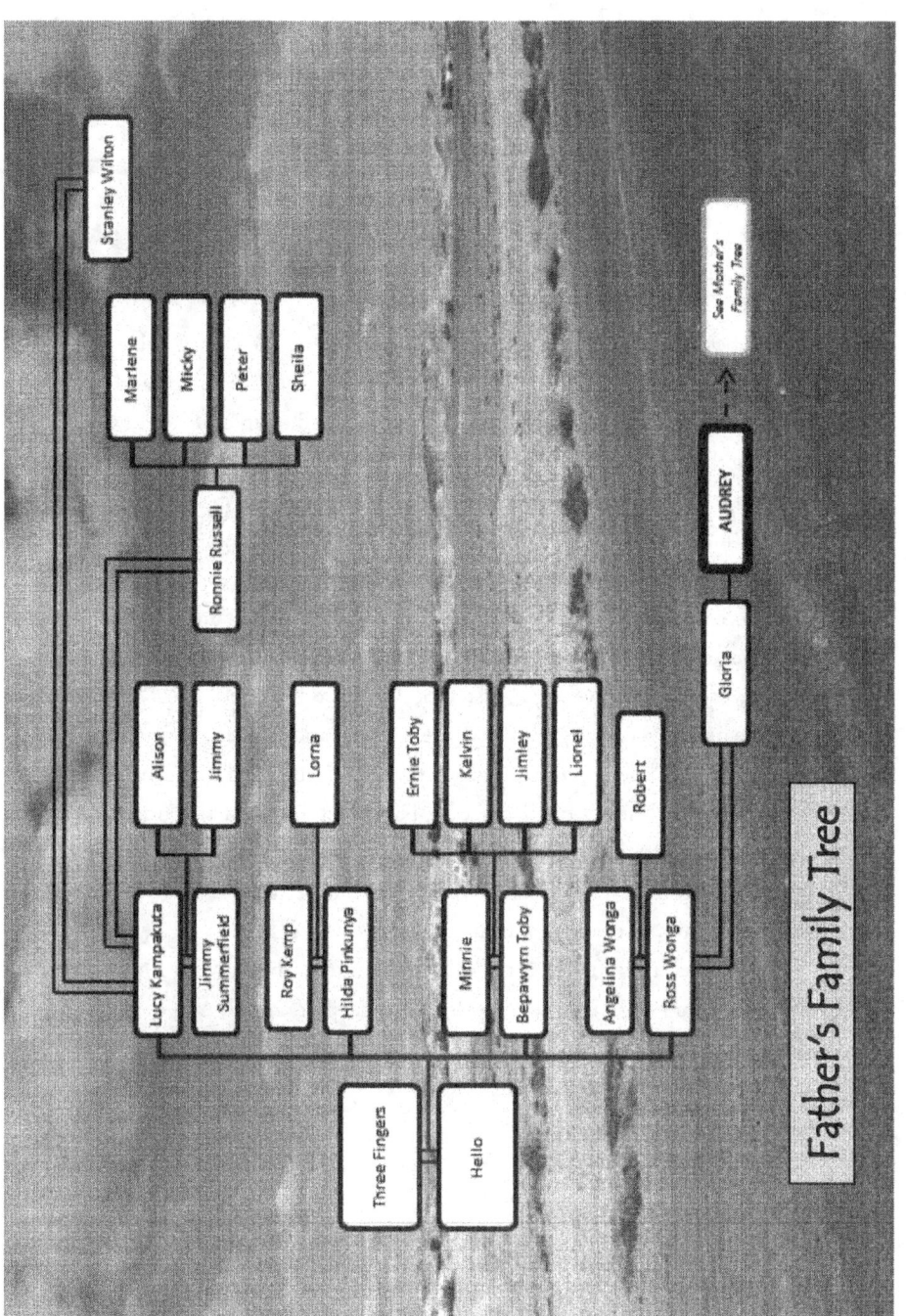

on Indian Hill. Then Alinta shifted up on the side of this hill here, so I asked for a transfer to House Number One on Umoona because this house has a lot of memories. I grew up in this house with Uncle Barney and Aunty Dorothy. And it's walking distance to my grandkids – they can come up here.

I sit out here and watch the cars coming from Oodnadatta, see what's happening on the Reserve. Sometimes we spot *kanyalas* on the hill there. That's rock wallabies, *kanyalas*.

I've been in the Ambulance for two years now. Here in Coober Pedy. I'm doing it to help my people. Sometimes when they're sick and they see the ambulance, they might shy down – shut up and not say anything. But when they see a family member, they all open up and tell me what it is. Everyone knows I'm in it.

In 2008, I went to Marree for the handover. They were handing over some land to the Dieri people. I was invited to go to help the Sister – Sister June. There were going to be over a thousand people there. Sister June's been there for many years working in the hospital there. Everyone calls her *Kaku*, Sister. So I went to help her.

I'm a bus driver now. I'll be fifty-one this year and last year I wanted a job that I could do and they needed a bus driver but I had no licence. I had a licence but no bus licence so I went in and said to Forrest Holder, who's our Umoona Community CEO, 'Hey, Forrest, if I get my licence before a week, can I be the school bus driver?'

And he said, 'Go on – go for it!'

So I started training for it that afternoon and within a week I had my licence. So I drive the bus to pick up the kids for school. And every Monday we have a women's group. And Tuesdays we have a play group – pick them up. It's good little pocket money and it suits me and it's good to help get the kids to school.

I'm still on the Umoona Council. I was a councillor and then I got nominated to be a vice chairperson.

This week I'll be in Port Augusta for the interpreting course and my name will be on a register – interpreters' register. If someone needs me,

Audrey and her family. L to R: Ray-Ray, Kyren (peeping), Ronald, Audrey, Alinta and Kailon, Benji, Patricia and Tyrell. (Audrey Wonga private collection)

Jason. (Audrey Wonga private collection)

they can get my name and phone number and if anyone needs me, I'll be ready to help. People coming down from the north – from the APY Lands in the courthouses if they do something wrong or silly – if they need legal advice, it's not me giving legal advice, it's me breaking the language barrier. Without that, without that interpreting, people couldn't understand, they say yes to something they didn't do or did. They say, '*Uwa, uwa,* yes, yes' and don't know what they're saying yes to.

And in hospitals again, the interpreting comes in handy for that – when they have to have an operation, you make sure they get their arm cut off, not their leg!

Audrey at Coober Pedy. (Photo courtesy of Michele Madigan)

My last word

I hope my story encourages young people with something I've said in my book. You know, to keep the language up, always think about your other family and friends – like in joining the Ambulance, doing training. Look at me – I'm half a century but I'm still doing these things! You're never too old to do anything. I got my bus licence at fifty – I did have it years ago but I let it go. But because I wanted a job, just a bit of extra cash and helping kids get to school. My grandson's started school so he camps over here on school days and I get him up early and go and pick up the bus. *Palya*!

Epilogue

I'm a qualified interpreter now. I'm on the interpeters' register. I passed my certificate through TAFE, going to Port Augusta for the interpreters' course. I'm going to Adelaide in April for graduation to receive my certificate. I've got my ABN number and I'm getting cards made up. I've applied to Centrelink and the hospital. They're having the course in Coober Pedy this year so the Oodnadatta mob can come over for it.

In November 2009, I was voted in as Umoona chairperson for Umoona Community Council. I have to represent Umoona Community Council and Umoona Community to the government and other organisations. I need to be there in the Umoona office to sign letters and to register Umoona Council mail and do all the other things needed to be done by the chairperson. I'm happy that I'm a local woman that's been recognised. The older I get, the wiser I'm being!

Yes, like the Bible says: 'Seek and you shall find.'

Word list

Antikirinya/Yankunytjatjara	English
Anangu	an Aboriginal person
Dunjiba	Oodnadatta – literally the 'Township'
inyurpa	of the opposite generation moiety
kaku	sister – affectionate term
kamuru	uncle – mother's brother or close male cousin, her brother-in-law
kangkuru	older sister or female cousin
kanyala	euro or hills kangaroo
katja	son, woman's sister's son, man's brother's son
kulini	listening, understanding
kumana or kumanara	literally 'no name' – the name people are given when a person with the same name passes away
kuna	poo, faeces
kungka	woman
kuntili	aunty –father's sister or close female cousin, his sister in law
malany	younger sister or brother, cousin
mama	dad, daddy, father; father's brother, his close male cousin

mangata	quondong
ngunytju	mum, mummy, mother; mother's sister/close female cousin
pakali	grandson, great nephew
palya	good, OK, all right
puliri	granddaughter, great niece
punu	tree, bush, wood
tjamu	grandfather, great uncle, (can be) grandchildren
tjilpi	old man, elder
tjulpu	bird
uwa	yes
waltjapiti	family
walypala	whitefella
wangka	language, word
wangka kulini	understanding the language
wararakati!	get off, jump down!

Reference

Goddard, Cliff (compiler). *Pitjantjatjara/Yankunytjatjara Dictionary*, IAD Press, Alice Springs. 1996.

You Have To Survive Somehow

Brian Strangways
(Kokatha)

Dedicated to my mum, Eva Strangways

and also Mr and Mrs Mac.

Early days

I'm Brian Strangways, born the first of the seventh month, 1946, Port Augusta, on Umeewarra Mission. I was born out in the open. I'm the youngest out of four boys, two eldest sisters and two youngest sisters. I'm the only boy left, with three girls – the older one living in Victoria, married to a Scotsman, the two younger ones back in Port Augusta. The two youngest ones are Eileen and Lynette. Kathleen is married to Walter Lang in the Dandenongs. The eldest sister Thelma passed away.

The old mission, this is the one everyone was talking about – before they shifted up to where Umeewarra stands today. I was born not far from there and Susie Reid, God bless her soul (she's gone now), she was the midwife. Yes, I was born on the *manta*, the earth. All of us kids, according to Mum, were born in the bush, not in the hospital. Mum was trying to get over there to this first Mission house – but I couldn't wait and she didn't get there! But Susie Reid was there.

Yes, Mum and Dad were married. We called them Mum and Dad. We weren't allowed to call them by their first names. Call the grandparents *Tjamu* – Grandfather, Nana… If you called them by

First Mission house, Umeewarra. (Photo courtesy of Mrs Ivy McWilliams)

Dad, Tim Strangways, is holding the horse. Johnny next to him, I would have been on the breast, in the dray somewhere with Mum, Eva Strangways. Lofty was the name of the lead camel.
(Photo: Len Beadell. Aboriginal heritage, DOSAA.
At East Well on Coondamba Station, 1950.)

their first names then, in those days, oh, he'd take the belt off! In those days, they had discipline. Nowadays, kids call their parents by their first names.

In Umeewarra

Then Mum and Dad split, so we were all put in the Home –Umeewarra. I don't think John, the oldest brother, was in the Home. Just me and Cyril and Leo. We did see Mum after that but we were still in the Home. Miss Simmons, she was in charge, the overall boss, then Miss Cantle, and Miss Morton was the medical – she was the nursing sister. Miss Simmons, Miss Cantle and Miss Morton, the original missionaries, they lived in the first house.

In the house, the boys' room was called the Green Room and the girls' room was called the Pink Room. And Miss Simmons used to have the room on her own and Miss Cantle and Miss Morton were one, each side of the boys and the girls. Supervising. The girls was on the right and the boys on the left and Miss Simmons's room was on

From left: Grandmother Ruby (Egan), Mum Eva, that's me – Brian – I was the youngest. Then in front: Cyril (passed on), eldest brother Johnny, Grandfather Ted Egan (not the singer) with the biggest hat on, second to oldest brother Leo at the back on the camel cart, and I'm not too sure but I think Hector Lang. The other fellow I can't recall (Tommy Martin or Sid Strangways). I don't think my Dad is in this photo. Nellie Lang is fourth from the left.
(Photo: SA Museum.)

the left too. She was up in the front because she did all the brain work – she was like the accountant, running the show. The missionaries – like Miss Simmons, the head lady – they weren't qualified teachers but she had to do all the bookwork to run the place with the government. There was only one teacher, Miss Cantle. Other than that, there were no qualified teachers there in my time. The other missionary, Miss Morton, she was a nurse.

With the help of the government, they built up the home. I didn't know about those kind of things in those days of course. They put the kitchen on one side of the main house. Then the dining room. Then they built the boys' dormitory on the other side and then the girls' dormitory was straight out from there. When I was only a little kid, I used to go down to Melrose for the holidays – that was before the Macs came.

Before Mr and Mrs Mac, was Mr and Mrs Thomas – Neil Thomas, I think. And then another couple came in – the Irish couple there, Martin. See, they'd just come out to do their little couple of years mission there.

The Umeewarra people, they took us kids from the Home to Whyalla to see the Queen (March 1954). We were right in front there. There I was on the front page of the Whyalla newspaper – or it might have been the *Advertiser* – a little boy from Umeewarra Mission holding the flag. Yes, Union Jacks in those days – no Australian flag. A lot of hogwash! I didn't know what the Queen was and what it was all about. We just went for a school trip – I didn't know anything about it! Just there waving my flag – the Union Jack. Just calling out what we told to say. Yes, Union Jacks before we went into school, they used to pull the Union Jack up. 'I am an Australian, I am a British subject…' – hogwash! We just said what we were told to say.

When Mr and Mrs Mac (he was better known as Mr Mac), first came, they wouldn't have been too many years older than I was. They were pretty young then; would have been in their twenties. 'Cause when I left there, I was fourteen years of age. They didn't have any children of their own then and to my knowledge they didn't have any after either. They branched out with the building. Mr Mac, he was

Mr and Mrs McWilliams – he was better known as Mr Mac.
(Photo courtesy of Mrs Ivy McWilliams)

a builder, so I gave him a hand. He started on the girls' dormitory. I worked on that till I got moved to Mount Barker. And after that they built another one there for babies, like – a nursery. I think that's been pulled down now because white ants got in there.

Stanley Lennon, Gordon Simmons, Dougie Waye, Darryl Taylor, Tiger McKenzie, Lionel Chimney, Charlie Jackson, Ian Waye, Adrian Hull, Russell Crombie, Harold Lang, Kingsley Stewart, Richard Waye, Sammy Brown – they were all at Umeewarra when I was there. But they all weren't in the Home – Umeewarra Home – but we all went to the same Mission School. It wasn't even Davenport then; it was just Umeewarra Mission. There were a couple of kids that came in that had to learn to speak English but they never got a smack or anything for speaking the lingo. Norah Kiltie, Andrew Kiltie's sister, was in the Home. Her mother came to visit her. I think Norah died in Coober Pedy. There were a lot of other girls there. I haven't seen them since and then they got married and… But there was Judy Rigney – she married a Nunga bloke, Tex Ferguson, from New South. And I think that she's up around that area there now – Coober Pedy. They separated.

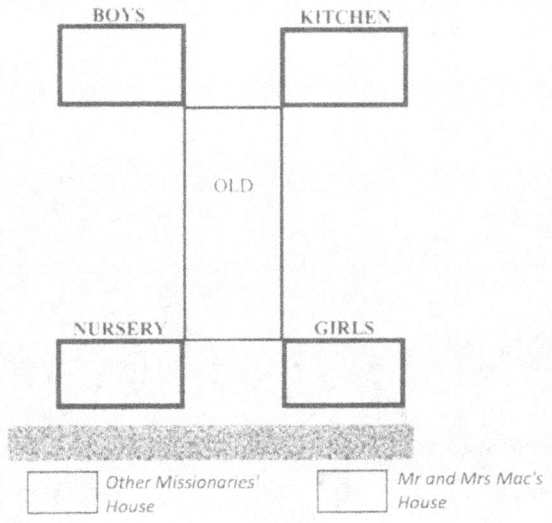

Umeewarra Mission, now on Davenport community, Port Augusta. Brian's sketch.

Marlene Reid, Ivy Barton – I think she's up in Alice Springs there now. So Aboriginal kids would all go to the Mission school. Later on, some of them did go into town there, like then mixing with the white kids – which is a good thing too.

When Davenport did get started, Barney and Jessie Lennon, and Syd Waye got the first two houses. Those two houses were next to the church. (Then Jessie and Barney split and later Jessie ended up with my brother Leo and they had Judy.) The church was a big corrugated-iron building – and I built that church with Mr Mac.

The other Christian mob would come down: tradesmen – all different trades, boiler makers, carpenters, bricklayers – for the weekend to give us a hand. So with Mr Mac and Mrs Mac, we finished the Home and we built the Gospel Hall just down from Umeewarra, on Davenport. Big congregation – mainly all Aboriginal people on the Mission. So I helped Mr Mac do that.

We had another house there at Umeewarra – that's where Mr and Mrs Mac used to live. And then when I was there, I helped Mr Mac build their own house when I was fourteen, when I left school. This was the first house we built before we started on the girls' dormitory. It was an asbestos house and my brother Cyril and Mr Mac and, see,

Umeewarra Mission house. 'That's Mr Mac's car.'
(Photo courtesy of Mrs Ivy McWilliams)

every weekend, a Christian group used to come up from Adelaide – they'd call a working bee to help. Electricians, boilermakers… I think they call them Christian Brethren – it's Gospel Hall mob anyway. There was another house again – a house for visiting missionaries.

And from there, I went to Mount Barker. Yes, well, I don't know – they might have been sorry when I had to leave…

Getting back to that asbestos house, Mr and Mrs Mac's house: Mrs Mac, she ended up getting cancer. She passed away last year some time (2010). And my brother Cyril died of cancer too – cancer of the throat. But I think it had something to do with the asbestos. When we were building the house, we had to cut sheets of asbestos. (Yes, I've been following the Hardy case.) Cyril died when he was fifty-one, so it was thirteen years ago – he would have been sixty-four now – he's one year older than me.

On ration days, on a Friday, all these people would come in and get a box of rations – groceries, bread, tinned stuff. After we'd finished school, we'd help out – we'd fill a box from the stores for the families. And the medical dispensary was next to it.

Mr Mac's still alive. When Umeewarra closed, Mr and Mrs Mac bought a property down at Cowell. See, there's a Christian mob down there too: Whyalla, Cowell – they used to come and help at Umeewarra

Ration day on a Friday at the old shed on Umeewarra.
(Photo courtesy of Mrs Ivy McWilliams)

L to R: Ruby McKenzie (Marree mob), Kathleen Hull and my mum, Eva Strangways (née Egan), probably in the Flinders Ranges somewhere. (Brian Strangways private collection)

too. They'd take kids down there for holidays and that. Cyril and I went on a farm out there for holidays because we didn't go where the other kids went for Christmas holidays – we stayed back and helped Mr Mac with the building. When everyone else came back, we went down to Cowell then for holidays. That was OK. Later, when I'd left school (you see, the other kids were going to school), and we decided to stop around and give Mr Mac a hand with the building. On the holidays at Cowell, we didn't do much – just go and give Bill Tonkin a hand mustering sheep and do a bit of shearing and that. We liked that. The farm was just out of Cowell – the Tonkin family.

Not very often, but we did see our mum. About every eighteen months, they'd come back to Port Augusta, stay there for a while and go back out to the stations for work. My stepdad and my mum used to come back just to see us and then go back out to the stations. My stepdad was Cassidy – he was actually my youngest sister, Lynette's father. I'm not sure if he was Arabunna too. But they could all speak the same lingo. He had a couple of brothers, but they died. Missed our mum but once you got used to everybody else, the rest of the kids – they were family. One big family. And all of my own brothers except Johnny and all of my sisters except Lynette and Eileen were in the Home as well. Wally Crombie and Russell (Crombie) were there too. (I don't know about Russell – if he's still kicking or what...) I know them all. But all the kids, they all weren't in the Home. But we all went to the Mission School; it wasn't Davenport then. People were just living on Umeewarra.

We saw our dad as well. He used to come and visit and give us lollies, lemonade – something like that. We'd sit on the veranda, or in the garden, in the shade. They used to come back when they could. My eldest sisters were in the Home. They were the good ones; they went over to Singleton Training College in NSW. It was a Bible College – so a few of the girls used to go there. The eldest sister Thelma met up there with the bloke she married – he was a Johnson, Bernard Johnson. They settled in Bundaberg, Queensland, because that's where Bernie Johnson come from. He was a Kanak – they'd bring 'em over (his parents) a long time ago, more or less as slave labour to be cane cutters.

I've been over to Bundaberg to see them two or three times. I took Mum over there for the funeral – my sister's funeral. My sister had been on the kidney dialysis thing. I'd just left there about three days before she passed away and then I had just got back to Port Augusta and there was a knock at the door – Mr Mac. My brother Cyril was there too.

'Sit down outside there,' and he told us the bad news that Thelma had passed away.

Then I was the one nominated to take Mum back over there for the funeral because the others hadn't been over there. Well, I was the one that moved around – I was the rolling stone. Three days after I got back and I had to go all the way back over there and bring Mum back. It was a long trip on the stupid bus. I don't think the others – the other youngest sisters and Cyril (he was still alive) – they'd never been over there! They'd just been around Port Augusta, Coober Pedy, the other stations – back and forward, just like that. I'd been around more than the others. Plus I was used to it with my work – moving around.

Yes, I reckon I am a bit more adventurous. I've been in most states and I don't think my other two sisters or my brothers have been out of our state. My niece lived along the Nullarbor and that was about it for her – moved back to Port Augusta. Yeah, I like moving around – to see what's over the next hill, what's around the next corner. I shacked up a couple of times myself with somebody. But that never worked, 'cause like I say, I like to move around. Not be tied down.

Dad died when I was in Alice Springs – he was well into his seventies. I was in my twenties then. My dad had some brothers up around Marree way but I never got to know them. He had sisters too – one was Clara Hull. She used to be Strangways. Clara's daughter married into the Hodgsons from up in Darwin. He was a Scotsman – Geordie Hodgson. Came to Darwin. They're connected to us because their grandmother was a Strangways. Yes, I'm Arabunna through the Old Man.

My mum was Kokatha. She was an Egan. Mum was in her seventies too when she passed away. It took a while to get back to speaking the language. When I was a little kid, I don't think I spoke English – I just spoke my parents' lingo. Then at Umeewarra, there we were young kids and you tend to forget the lingo, speaking English all the time. I can't speak the language all through nowadays but still understand it. Don't speak any here in Murray Bridge but I speak some when I'm in Port Augusta. Other than that I haven't had much to do with it all, language and that – with the Mission and then with moving all the time.

In the Boys' Home

They only took boys till about fourteen, something like that, at Umeewarra. Then I was put in the Mount Barker Boys' Home. I went there in about 1960. There was three other boys from Umeewarra, we come through there. And there was a few from Whyalla and Iron

Knob. There was Clifford Bramfield – he's passed on. Peter Ward, Teddy Johns – he passed on. Johnny French. That's about the only ones I knew from Port Augusta.

It was bad there at Mount Barker; you weren't free – nothing. At Umeewarra we were free – you could walk, go anywhere. But in Mount Barker you couldn't go anywhere – it was farm country. No good for a bush kid. I had an altercation with the captain – punched him in the head. And away I went! Yes, don't worry – they had the cops out for me. But I walked all the way down to Murray Bridge, got a job for the day painting forty-four-gallon Shell petrol drums. Got on the train, the old steam train to Adelaide. Caught that other train from there a couple of hours later and headed back to Port Augusta. And that was it – I got away! You have to survive somehow.

In Port Augusta, saw my mum, Eva Strangways, and my dad, Tim Strangways, and my brothers – they were alive then. Mum was bringing up Judy, that's Jessie Lennon's daughter. Judy's father was my second oldest brother, Leo. I hadn't seen the family when I was in Mount Barker. It wasn't that I was so homesick for family. I just wanted to get away from over here – it was bad. It was more oppressive than anything else – in the Home. Think it was '62, '63.

Working life on the Oodnadatta Track

And from there, I got a job making bricks. Stayed there about six months. Left that and joined the Railways. Most of my time I spent with the Railways. I did a bit of lying there too – at that time you had to be twenty-one, so I just bunged my age up a bit, gave a dodgy age. I was about the same size as I am now, fairly tall but a bit thinner. Well, they didn't worry anyhow because they wanted blokes out, to stay out bush to maintenance the track so they weren't too worried about that you were telling lies or not. It was hard to get single blokes – that's because there was nothing out there. I was about seventeen at the time.

I went to a place called Beresford, up there by Marree; Oodnadatta wasn't too far off. We were working on the line, I'm talking about the narrow gauge going up to Alice Springs. You could walk faster than the narrow 3 foot 6 inch train! It was built before my time! It didn't have all the ballast for the rails – it was just laying on sand. You'd dig a trench, put a sleeper in there, spike it down. Yes, it was mainly all sand. In the 1800s, the Afghans on camels were carting all the sleepers to make the track. They even took part of the bridge here – from Murray Bridge, out there. Because when they shifted it out from England, they were thirty-five feet short. Back in those days, they didn't have all the technology you've got now – otherwise they would have just welded the thing together. So they shipped part of the bridge up by steam train across the creek. Algebuckina bridge (1,922 feet 3 inches, just over half a kilometre) it's, well, that's where that bridge is from – here, Murray Bridge.

It's just sitting there now. There's no rails – the railway moved over west. (Tarcoola to Alice Springs.) So the bridge is just sitting there now. It's a tourist attraction there now. You can go up there through William Creek, up through to Oodnadatta. Or back the other way from Coober Pedy.

Yes, it was at Tarcoola siding, later on (1981), that they brought in the standard rail gauge (4 foot 8½ inches) going to Alice Springs when they got rid of the narrow gauge over at Beresford, Warrina, Oodnadatta – on that eastern side. I was still in the Railways but I didn't have much to do with the new line – the standard gauge from Tarcoola to Alice Springs. It was too sandy on the Central Australian Railway – that's what it was known as – and it flooded everywhere, round through Marree, Beresford. We used to get a lot there in William Creek – you used to get washaways. The train would just have to sit there – you couldn't go forward and you couldn't go back till it dried out a bit. They had to send gangs up there to fix it up.

There are a couple of the old diesel trains parked at Marree now, just for the tourists. After they got rid of the diesel trains (they were narrow gauge), that's when they got these NSUs – I think that was the brand name for the locomotives diesels. Those old diesels are obsolete

*The old NSU diesel on the narrow gauge to Alice Springs.
(Photo: R. Pearce. AIATSIS.)*

now so they just parked them over at Marree. The first locomotive diesel that came in was GM1 on the standard gauge side from Port Augusta to Kalgoorlie – it done a million miles without any spanner or anything put to the engine.

Well, at Beresford, back when I was seventeen, you'd get up at half past seven and get on the machine – the little section car – a little trolley sort of thing, which'd take you to work and bring you back. Then you'd come home. Then you'd sit down and play cards or something like that. Not that I'm a gambler – I still don't understand how to play cards. I had an old guitar and that was it – mouth organ, singalong. You had to make your own social life – you've got nowhere to go. There was plenty of grog drunk there. Well, at that time we weren't allowed to drink – the Aboriginal people weren't allowed to drink until Don Dunstan came into power and opened the gates for everyone. But there was drinking out there – the white people had plenty of beer. Everyone was still all on deck next morning.

The bosses: we had one – he wasn't much. He was one of these stand-over merchants. But everyone else, we all got in together. All of us were single blokes. But there were camps up there with married people – Oodnadatta, Marree – that's about it. Towards Port Augusta they had married camps – about six houses. A few miles south of Warrina – it was miles in those days – was Edwards Creek. Edwards

Creek was a married camp – four houses and a single camp as well – I was there too. It was better known as 'Dodge City' instead of Edwards Creek. When I went there, they had an old Winchester rifle nailed on top of the railway destination board. 'Dodge City'! – because they used to shoot and hang them, the blokes who are working there. There's a little graveyard out from there – Warrina graveyard. Well, there was no cops around. There's nothing much to do, so get into an argument there and up with the rifle. That was before my time, though. There were fights, though, in my time – just with the fists. That used to happen a lot because you used to get sick of looking at each other, arguments start and…playing cards or anything like that and someone started cheating… And she's on!

I was young, yes, but I was okay because I wasn't too bad with these things – my fists. In the Home, you've got to fight or you're always going to be picked on all the time, especially at that place there – Mount Barker. In the Mount Barker Home, we Aboriginal boys, we were ruling the roost! You don't want to be bullied or picked on and you stand up and fight and the best man come out on top! If you couldn't, well, you'd be stood on all the time.

Abminga was the last camp on the old narrow gauge line on the South Australian border before you cross the border into the Northern Territory – I've been there a few times, you know, working.

Then there was Duffield in the Territory – been through there a few times going to Alice Springs. But we'd meet up there on the end of the line and then go back and work. And then there was Finke – Finke Hotel – there was a hotel and a camp. Just visiting there on payday! No work.

Then I left the job. But you get sick of doing nothing and then you go to into the job again and they send you anywhere – it's a walk-up start in those days. And from there, I went up to Alice Springs. No transfer – in those days, it was a walk-up start. There was plenty of work around. Like I said, you walk up and bang, you've got a job. Not like these days now.

After I left Alice Springs, I went back to Port Augusta and I was in the workshop for a while before I was transferred to the welding gang and went out bush to Loongana on the Nullarbor and stayed on it for about eleven months.

The move to Darwin

Well, I've been up to Darwin – drive trucks, machinery… I wasn't always with the Railways, but the Railways was the mainstay, more or less in my working days. But I knew a couple of blokes from there who had come down to play football at Port Augusta. That's where I met 'em. I was playing for West Augusta and they were playing for Souths.

So they said, 'Well, come up to Darwin there. Play up there. The footy season's on there. Well, when that finishes you start rugby.'

Got a job there in Darwin with the council. The games were going all along – rugby, Aussie rules and basketball and all that – but I wasn't into basketball. More or less you go out there training and the selectors look at you and you sign up; you're one of the players. Playing footy in Darwin, it'd be hot, steamy. The next half an hour, a thunderstorm would come and you'd run around ankle deep in water. They didn't play any different, only it was the heat. Heat and humidity. Down here in South Australia, Port Augusta footy was on all winter time – it was cold.

On the way from Darwin to Alice Springs.
(Photo courtesy of Mary Pullen)

A long time after that, I was up in Darwin again. Every year, they'd send a gang of people up there to Darwin for six months; it was Commonwealth – or National Railways. There were that many titles to it. (I think it's called Great Southern Railways now. I'm not sure whether it's English, Japanese or Canadian now.) So the last time I was in Darwin, it was from being sent up in the Railways. They sent me up that last time from on the Nullarbor. A couple went on the plane from Adelaide and three of us drove up by car right through from Port Augusta. We finished our time with the Railways in the gang there in Darwin about a week and a half before Tracey come through! We drove down to Alice Springs and then we put our cars on the train to Port Augusta. We had to drive to come back to our original place there on the Nullarbor.

Life on the Nullarbor

On the Nullarbor, I was one of the welders. One of the workers, Paul Hinch, took those photos of me on the East–West line, out on the Nullarbor. Welding isn't a trade, it's just a semi skilled job. You'd have

Brian welding on the Nullarbor, stage 1. 'The steel is beginning to boil and bubble.' (Photo courtesy of Paul Hinch)

to be fit to go out in the rail gangs in the first place. But I think it was this bending over to chip the excess steel off the rail, top and both sides that injured my back and knees, ankles, elbows – every joint. Hot in summer time and cold in the winter. The good thing about it was the heat from the welding pot in winter; everybody else wanted to be offsider then, handing you all your chisels and putting down the sand moulds. One bloke's got to be on this side and the other bloke has to be on the other side and we'd seal it up with volclay, otherwise the molten steel would go straight through, burning a big hole and you'd have to start all over again with another forty-foot-long rail. Lifting the rail too – you'd do your back in too.

'Protection of life and property' – that was the first two rules in the Railways. If you wanted to be a ganger or a track foreman, you'd have to study up to get your safe working ticket. I was offered that but I knocked it back. Too much back-stabbing. I said, 'I'll just do the work.'

Oh, it wasn't much on the Nullarbor. It was the same set-up. You couldn't go anywhere. You just had to stay home. We were living in old carriages – just for the welding gang – about ten or eleven of us in the gang. They got hot and cold showers and everything like on flat

'Molten steel already been poured out between the rails to seal it up. Poking the steel rod to keep the hole open.' 1970s. (Photo courtesy of Paul Hinch)

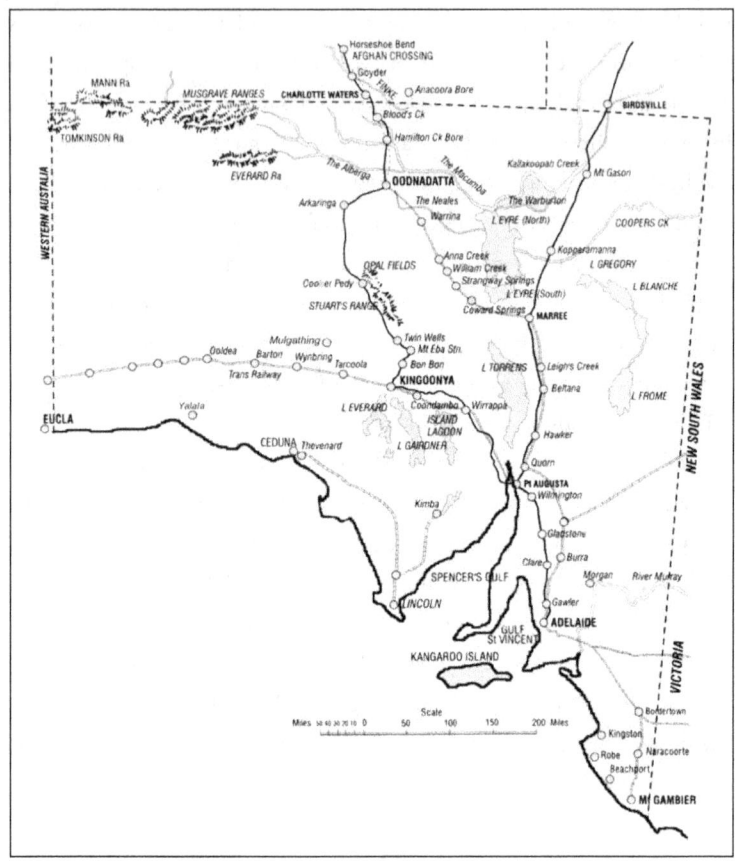

From the Tourists' Road Guide for South Australia, published by the National Roads Association of Australia (SA Branch) c1927. Thanks to Phil Hanley.

tops. Brought in those mobile huts and that. There'd be a few carriages there too. You'd have the main track there and on the line, off the main track, there'd be two loops where the trains crossed and we'll be in the furthest one away from the main track crossing. You've got the loop in every camp – the trains got to cross or pass. We had our own vehicles to go to the job site for that day.

We did come back down to Kingoonya – yes, we did transfer back down there to Kingoonya. But before that, we were right over on the Western Australian side – Loongana. Of course we went through all the sidings – Kingoonya, Wilgena, Tarcoola, Malbooma, Lyons,

Wynbring, Barton, Immarna, Ooldea, Watson, O'Malley, Cook, Denman, Hughes, Deakin, Reid, Forrest – to get to there, Loongana. Once you finish one section, they shift you up to the next camp – at Forrest.

That's where they had the airport at the time of Maralinga, the Maralinga bombs. And the pilots were ordered to fly through the radiation mushroom clouds!

At sidings like Langoona and Forrest, we always had plenty of money because you couldn't spend it out there, unless you ordered beer and other stuff from the store. You couldn't walk down to the corner store... (I did get a couple of cars later on with the money – but that didn't last too long.) There was only a fettlers camp at them sidings, that's all there was. Except for Cook – they had a school and a hospital and souvenir shop as part of the railway station. And the Club Room – where you could party on. On the weekends, we'd get on the train and head down for Cook. These days, drivers and crews on to the Indian Pacific as it's called now, still change at Cook. Going west, the WA crew takes over there, and going east, the South Australian crew take the train straight through to Port Augusta and on to Adelaide. But the engine changeover happens at Kalgoorlie. They unhook the engine, the diesel locomotive, at Kalgoorlie. They hook the other engine on and it goes right through then to Perth.

At the sidings down from where we were as workers handling the track, they had accommodation for the workers and their families. The women survived all right; you've got to make your own social life. Pay day there, they'd all have a barbecue. When the kids grow up a bit and they've got to go to school and that, that's when they leave. They've got to get a transfer to Port Augusta or the nearest place where there was a school – like Kingoonya or Rawlinna or Cook. Rawlinna, that's on the Western Australian side. My niece Judy and her husband were there. I went out there to see them after I came back from Queensland, a long time after I left the Railways.

I can't say on the Nullarbor I ever saw any of the Aboriginal people walking around there in the bush as we went past. In Kalgoorlie – we'd go in there from Loongana from boredom – you'd see plenty of them there. As you go past some places – like Coonana in WA – you'd see a lot of them there waiting for trains. I've jumped the trains a few times myself from Marree to Alice Springs when I wasn't working for the Railways. What you have to do is make sure you've got a couple of loaves of bread, tins of bully beef and water – flagons of water. You had to have them. You look at the destination ticket on the railway truck. If it's going to Alice Springs, you get on that as it's taking off. You've got to find out what times the train is going – the freight train. You wouldn't get on the passenger. And in the Railways there's only three times they run on – the right time, the wrong time and any time. And mainly any time. Yes, mostly any time!

When I was back at the Nullarbor, I got a letter telling me to take my leave – hadn't taken my leave for three years. So after that – three or four weeks – I went back to the Nullarbor. Then we shifted camp out to Kingoonya. The bosses of the Railways were heading west and they got off at Kingoonya that Sunday night. I fronted up for work with a can of beer in my hand and the boss told me to roll up my swag. It was on a pay day and the Tea and Sugar was coming going west, so I got paid off and I walked across the platform with the carton of beer and went back to the camp. There were a couple of people leaving in the car to go to Port Augusta so I jumped in the car with them. I was told I should have waited there till I got a letter from them. But I just took off.

And down south to Pimba

A couple of weeks later on, sitting down in the hotel there at Port Augusta, I heard on the news that one of the welding gangs got cleaned up by a goods train – a freight train, coming back from the west. Control gave them the okay for the section car to go to work at the sandhill there – I think it was at Barton where it happened, the other side of Tarcoola. I think there were just a few huts there for the workers. They would have been crossing left in the little section car. None of them got killed but later on they got compensated for it. So I was in the pub in Port Augusta, listening to the news then and got on the phone and rang the engineer – I went to the top – and said, 'I just heard about that this mob just got cleaned up.'

He sent me into see Mr Green. Don Green was the civil engineer: 'You can go and see Mr Green there now.'

Mr Green, he was the chief worker there, and he said, 'Well, okay, just come around to the office and we'll see what we can do.'

He said okay and I went to Pimba. Yes, a couple of hours later they sent me out to Pimba. From there, I went out to Wirrappa, the work place where we would start from to put the new rails down. There was a shift down to Wirrappa just down south from Pimba. Wirrappa was only a little railway camp, fettlers camp – about three or four houses there. It's just this side of Woomera. They had a stockpile of ballast there – that sort of thing for the track going there. So I started again with them! I knew they'd be short-handed – they wanted welders. And so I went out there just a couple of weeks later after leaving Kingoonya. One of the gang that was in the train smash died later on – in Adelaide, I think. The second one left the Railways. He was one of the ones that really got damaged in the smash. This would have been well into the '70s.

We were at the other side then and when a couple of jobs had to be done at Wirrappa we had to come down and do it and then go back to Pimba. We were based at Pimba at the time. When there were bad tracks, they used to ask us welders to go down there and put in some new rails and straighten the thing out. We had flat-top trolleys to put the rails on the section car and take the rails down to the job site; flat-top trolleys, Toyotas, Land Rovers and everything – we had everything laid on to get to places. They had fettlers camps all along the line for the workers handling the track. I'm talking now standard gauge on the East–West line.

One of the fellows from Kingoonya there, he wanted…he asked if

Kingoonya Hotel. (Photo courtesy of Fr Tony Redden)

I wanted to swap, so I went back to Kingoonya there. He came down to Wirrappa because he was just about ready to get married.

The Kingoonya Hotel – I knew that! We had a few parties there at Kingoonya. Got drunk a few times – especially when the Kingoonya races were on.

That's the time when everybody came together. The last time I heard, it was run by a bloke who was a 'roo shooter – Les White. And he also took over the store. That's a few years ago…

So, after Pimba, I swapped to Kingoonya. Then I shifted from Kingoonya down to Wirraminna. There were all empty houses at Wirraminna – we had our own mobile homes. We'd be working on one section of the line and then it'd be getting too far for us to travel backwards and forwards so they'd shift us up further. So we couldn't live in these houses at Wirraminna and they were all empty! These days, if the squatters were here looking for a place to stay, they could have went out there and bingo, they could fill them all. Soon after, they just demolished all those houses – the whole lot – because we done all the welding, and the gang came behind with concrete sleepers, and they didn't need us out there any more. So they just flattened them all there, all those houses, and pushed them over and burnt them. You could have bought them cheap, like four or five hundred dollars – but then you've got to transport them. And none of the fellas didn't have that kind of money.

Anyway this day, a new ganger came up and I walked across to the

Wirraminna Siding. (Photo: W. Tippett. Aboriginal Heritage, DOSAA.)

empty house at Wirraminna to fill the empty water containers up – they had plenty of rainwater in their tanks – and he took off without me. So I just left the things there and stayed in the camp there and he sent another one of the blokes back to pick me up. And I told him to get lost.

He come round himself and I told him the same thing and he said, 'You'll get transferred back down to Port Augusta to work in the yard there.'

And I said, 'That'll do me!'

So I went to the yard for a while and I didn't get the job down Port Germein there, being offsider with the other welder, so I left the Railways. I walked out and that was the finish of my job with the Railways.

After the Railways

After that, I went to Whyalla and got this job at BHP. It didn't take long to get it either. There was a big workshop there and I got a job there working in the yard and they just asked us, 'Does anyone want to work on the weekends and get holiday pay?'

It was a pallet plant, loading the ships up. Pulling levers – like, you know, getting the conveyor belt going ahead into the ship. They sent down the conveyor belts for the iron ore, iron ore dust. And other stuff they put into the big shed there and make it into balls, little pellets in the oven. Most of the stuff is just iron ore and with the dust, they dampen it and roll it into little balls and they put it in the oven. They send it back on the conveyor belt to us and we send it straight back on to the ships. To Japan, China, America, wherever they want iron.

Half of the blokes didn't want to do weekend or overtime so I took it up. Double pay – sixteen hours a day. We worked holidays. You had to get the boat loaded. A lot of the work was sitting down – listen to the siren. It was one siren for stop and two to start again. So you listened to that siren. The conveyor belt runs out to the jetty, runs out on the machinery – the bloke operating the machinery there. The belt moves up and down – it just runs up – with the iron ore into the hold of the ship.

I was at the Whyalla job twelve months, I think. Yes, double time pay. Long hours, dirty work. Dust!

'Jessie Lennon with my niece Judy.' Port Augusta, 1963.
(Photo courtesy of Mrs Ivy McWilliams)

Moving around...

I got sick of it then. I went back to Port Augusta and went down to Adelaide with enough money to keep me going for a few weeks after that time at Whyalla. I had been to Adelaide before visiting. This time I got on the dole. And from there, I ended up going to Bundaberg to see my nieces and nephews and from there went to Toowoomba, tordoning – poisoning the trees. We'd put an axe to them. It's a new version of ringbarking. Clearing the land for cattle grazing.

I think it's the work that's giving me all the pain today – because most of the jobs I've been doing is all the heavy stuff, you know. Cement, pick and shovel, builder's labourer and fencing – oh yeah. Driving trucks in Darwin. The same things are always the matter – pain in the hips from that job in Whyalla loading up the pallets on to the ships. Pulling levers like, you know. You get the conveyor belt going out to the ship. Iron ore! Dust! Iron stuff! Sixteen hours a day! Then when I was in the Port one time, I fell off a stool – it was a high stool too. I think I must have blacked out first. And I just landed on my back! Lucky I didn't bash my head on the cement floor there. And when I went to Toowoomba there, they put me on the pension. That was about 1986, something like that.

Another time, moving around, I travelled up to Coober Pedy just to visit when I had a car that time there, and stayed there at Coober Pedy a couple of nights. I went up there with Judy, my niece; she wanted to see her mother, Jessie – Jessie Lennon. Johnny Coulthard, Judy's husband came too. Coulthards, they come from up above Leigh Creek. Yes, we stayed a couple of nights and came back home to Port Augusta. I never stayed in Coober Pedy that much before – we just travelled through.

Got pinched then, driving no licence. Syd Waye and I, we were going to Stirling North to see a bloke I knew. Syd Waye (I think he's gone too), he was three times drunker than I was and the cops told him to take the car – I think he did have a licence but he was three times drunker than I was and they still let him take the car! Back home to his place. Well, they locked me up and then they had to take me down to Port Germein and meet the police from Pirie – they had to bring the machine up so I could blow in it, because their machine in Port Augusta wasn't working so they had to drive me down to Port Germein outside of Pirie there and the Pirie police came up with the machine and I had to blow in it. By that time, I was pretty well sober. Couldn't get a smoke off them, though – 'Wait till we finish.'

Blew in the machine and he said, 'Here you are – you can take one from there.'

There were three or four there and he was so busy writing so I helped myself. The Port Augusta coppers were still waiting there in a patrol car. Then they put me in the patrol car, took me back to Port Augusta, locked me up and let me go again next morning! Cost me about fifty or sixty bucks fine.

Yes, I've only been to jail for minor offences – like dodging fines, contempt of court, drinking. That was an offence for Aboriginal people – until the time Don Dunstan opened the gate. (I had a good little side business going in Port Augusta when I was playing for West Augusta and most of the coppers played for West Augusta; I used to go into the pub and drink – I was only eighteen at the time and we weren't allowed to drink. Well, no one was allowed to drink till they were twenty-one – white or black. And black – we weren't allowed to drink at all). About this time, I got a house in Port Augusta but got sick of that and went to Adelaide.

Adelaide

Yes, some of the time I'd go down to Adelaide – just for a while. Johnny, he had to go to hospital. That's how I met Sr Michele and Sr Ann – in Victoria Square there. Then I was visiting Johnny in hospital and in walks Sister Ann. And I went with George Rankine and Louise to a birthday party there at Fletcher Road, where Sister Ann and Sister Michele were staying. I stayed for a couple of weeks at George and Louise's. I think it was Michele's birthday – with one hundred candles! No, there was only one candle.

Another time, I boarded for a while with Doreen Wanganeen in Harrison Street because she was with Syd – Syd Chamberlain, who used to be with my cousin, another Kathleen Strangways.

After Whyalla, though, I left Port Augusta and just come down to Adelaide. A change! I'd just come down visiting before when I was working. Because I'd been there before, I didn't notice the change much – it wasn't really much difference.

When I did go down to Adelaide to live, it was hot weather, so I'd just sleep out in the park. There was the (Aboriginal) Sobriety there on South Terrace. Marshall Carter was the manager there. I stayed at the Sobriety Group Cyril Lindsay Hostel for a couple of weeks. I came up here, Murray Bridge to Kalparrin. Just stayed a couple of weeks and I got drunk, so they called the cops. They didn't charge me, though, so the next day I went back and got my stuff and then I went back to Cyril Lindsay.

Working with Sister Janet Mead's mob

And from there, bumped into another bloke, Dave Wilkes, I used to work with on the line, a long time back. He took me down to Sister Janet Mead's and I was working there, working in the garden there, at the Adelaide Jail Garden. Before I came on the scene, she bought that land or leased it at the old Adelaide Jail and turned it all into a garden – growing all the vegetables, fruit trees...

A couple of weeks after that, they got me a flat – in Claxton Street, in the city, just off of Gouger Street there. The accountants there, they used to get you a house, and you'd get it a lot quicker than a Housing Trust house! Through MACHA: Multi Accommodation Community Housing. Michelle was the accountant; the accountants were responsible for getting houses – places for their workers. And I stayed with them there for two or three years there, living in the flat, working in the garden there. I did a bit of shovelling in the garden – and digging trenches – it wasn't that heavy.

Gina was the boss in the garden. She used to go to Selby Street and

Adelaide Jail Garden. L to R: Danny, Brian, David Wilkes, Mick, John Paech (dec). Gina in the background. (Brian Strangways private collection)

work in the clinic there with Damian – Damian Mead – on Fridays. Danny was the boss when Gina wasn't there. They were part of the Catholic mob as well. There was only mainly us mob there in the garden but sometimes they'd bring another couple of blokes down – like for building a cow shed there.

When we'd knock off work, I'd go and have a drink, but not much – we had to go and do that, that work next day. We used to go back to the centre – Moore Street. We didn't get paid, no, but we got everything we wanted at Moore Street – furniture, food, clothes there for nothing. I was on the pension by then. I got it when I was in Toowoomba there, about 1986. Before I did get the pension, I was more or less on sickness benefits – mainly for arthritis. I went to see a government doctor. He looked at me and said, 'Instead of all the time sickness benefits, I'll put you on the pension.'

It was a pretty good community, the Moore Street community. Yes, Sister Janet Mead's mob, they're all good people. There was Mick cooking there. He was an Irishman, you know. Michelle was the accountant. Louise and Phil. Another Mick was married to Gabby. Damian Mead – he's a doctor – was in a clinic in Selby Street, not far from where I was living in Claxton Street. I used to go to Damian to get my scripts. And Greg – Greg Mead – was a lawyer. Greg would come in round the place some times, have lunch and go back to work. Greg was a lawyer in the Children's Court in Wright Street.

And on my fiftieth birthday, they gave me a bit of a party (they gave it to everyone who had a birthday), and took some photos – of me and the workers. So it was the first of July '96. I'll be 65 this year, 2011!

There was a church around the corner from where I was in Claxton

Brian's fiftieth birthday, 1996. (Brian Strangways private collection)

Street – Westcare, they call it. You could go there and get a meal for two bucks: three-course meal for two bucks. If you haven't got two bucks, just get a bowl of soup, a pie and a pasty.

And then I left Claxton Street because I stopped working for them in Adelaide there – all the trouble with my leg and that. Another friend of mine, he used to come from Narrabri, I think – Shultz. I used to work with his brother, Cyril Shultz, a ganger in the railways, a long time back at Dodge City. Cyril, he ended up in Tasmania as a railway inspector. After he retired in Port Augusta, he got cancer of the eye. Don't know if he's still alive. He was an ex-Korea vet in the army. Anyway, Cyril's brother used to come down there to Adelaide from Mount Barker and he used to come and look me up. He used to sleep on my couch there in Claxton Street – 'Here, you can crash here.'

Well, he knew I was thinking about leaving the city. He rang me up two or three weeks later and said, 'There's a place up here at Mount Barker for sixty bucks a week.'

You had to buy your own tucker and that. Well, the landlord was Italian, Peter Barrolla – he had a place up there in Mount Barker, this side of the summit. He had a little hobby farm on the original Callington Road there and a place there that he turned into a boarding place for pensioners. He had his own little shop, a delicatessen down in Norwood or Magill in the city. His wife ran the shop and he'd come up to Mount Barker all the time, fixing the boarding place up. Sometimes he'd stay in the boarding house on the weekends. He had his own room there.

So I decided to move out of Adelaide and stayed there. There was an old bloke from Cherbourg there – well, he died and I took over payment of the car, an XD Falcon. It's a wonder I never got pinched – no licence and I been driving all over the place. (I had a licence in the Northern Territory, covered for everything – semis and heavy machinery. But I didn't get it renewed and then I left...)

But the place in Mount Barker was isolated and a lot of drink was going on there too. So then I put my name down at Murray Bridge at the Housing Trust for a flat and they ended up giving me this three-bedroom house here in Murray Bridge instead! They rung me up and told me. I got this house here in Murray Bridge after two months! That's all. I didn't know too many people in Murray Bridge but I knew Marshall was here. (Marshall's still there now 2011, at Kalparrin, Murray Bridge, but I think he's just shifted down to Mannum.) I ran into him again one day in Mount Barker in the chemist there to buy reading glasses. He'd swapped his Holden for a four-wheel drive he got from Mount Barker Toyota. He came behind me and tapped me on the shoulder: 'I've been trying to get hold of you.'

So when they rang me up from the Housing Trust to say I got the house, I rang Marshall up to come and pick my gear up – didn't cost me anything. He sent a truck up there. I didn't have much, mind you. I just had to wait for two weeks while they were painting the house and went to Vinnies, got a mattress and bed and small tables. Then I come and there were no lights so I had to go off and buy globes and that.

I've been in Murray Bridge ever since. Off pension week, I dry out for a while. Jeff has been out there at Kalparrin close to twenty years! He comes in here to the town and stays with me at the weekend. Because you're not allowed to drink out there. I've thought about having a garden here. But you can't grow anything here. You need a rotary hoe. Been fishing here but I don't go there – it's only a waste

Marshall knew my Mum in Andamooka.
'Aunty Eva Strangways was a beautiful person. She kept an eye on us all in Andamooka. On the west side of Andamooka her brother, Old Scotty Egan, and his wife lived in that car. To the right is the tin shed when Aunty Eva lived with Mr Cassidy.'
(Photo: Andrew Abbie, AIATSIS. Identified by Marshall Freeland Carter, Murray Bridge, 2011.)

of time. Tried it a couple of times and only got some small redfin. Someone else went and only got a couple of callop.

But I'm not thinking of going back to Port Augusta or anything. That's a wild place there now, so I've heard. Eileen my sister's talking about going back to Coober Pedy to stay. It's getting too rough for her. I'll go back and see them – for the weekend.

Ivan my nephew – Ivan Johnson originally from Bundaberg (Thelma's son but she's gone) – stayed here for a while. I came back home here one time from Adelaide and saw a note here on the door. He went down and booked into the Bridgeport and next day he came again and knocked on the door. Then I said, 'Go and get your gear out of the pub and stay here.'

He came and stayed for a while. He is a painter by trade. But he couldn't get a job around here and a mate here had wheels so we took the nephew from here, up there north. See, he couldn't get work around here and then he got a job in the mines and he's still up there. He got the job through Bungala, the CDEP mob in Port Augusta. There's a new mine this side of Coober Pedy – Prominent Hill – and he's still there. They stay out there a month now and get two weeks off. He's got himself some wheels so he'd drive the Commodore down to Port Augusta – because they got a couple of weeks off fully paid – he's making about three thousand bucks a week. Something like that.

He did come back here once. He was telling me he was a sample collector first. And now he's doing something else. And round that time, that was the last time I saw Kathy. My sister Kathy and Wally came and gave me a Crow's coat and a couple of shirts and socks. I used to ring Kathy up – tell her where I was. That's how Ivan found me because he was down in Victoria there. Then a couple of weeks back there was a knock on the door and who should be there but Lavina, Ivan's sister. With her bloke. She stopped here and showed me photos on a laptop thing of her side of the Johnson family and her kids and all this. And she asked me if I still had some photos.

But I said, 'Oh, don't ask me – they're all scattered here. I don't

L to R: Aleisha, Kale, Ashley and Reece. 2006.
(Brian Strangways private collection)

know where – in different drawers, cupboards… ' (Though there's that one I've got one of me on the Nullarbor…)

Lavina went up to Port Augusta then – saw her aunties and her other cousins, and Ivan of course. Lavina used to ring me up before she came.

Yes, Kathy brought me that Crows coat – I'm for the Crows – put your money on the Crows! I follow the football, Australian rules. Jimmy Steins, the Irishman, was the captain of Melbourne – he come out and won the Brownlow Medal and now he's got cancer. But he went on and took the young fella from Yuendemu back there and saw lots of good players there.

Slowing down a bit

I was going to leave here last year and go back to the hot country. But floods and cyclones… So I'm still here. Was going to Bundaberg – or Darwin. I've never been over to Broome – but once you get up that way, there are that many cyclones and heavy weather, round the coast… But you're not wearing heavy clothes like this – Murray Bridge, cold like this!

Well, one thing anyhow, now my leg and that, it's stopped me galloping all over the place you know, stopped me from travelling around 'cause I'm slowing down a bit. I can't go out and sleep out in the bush any more. Or catch a freight train – jumping it like I used to. Or hitchhiking. That's all over and done with! Since I've joined up with the Elders here in Murray Bridge, they got me the cleaner here – Lee Hutchinson. Helps with the floors, the bathroom.

Yeah, looking back over my life, what did Slim Dusty say? 'There's more dinner times than dinners!' And yes, I did work for a lot of the time too. In those days, you had to go and look for work. There was no dole around or anything like that, so you had to go and look for work. So when I ran away from that Boys' Home there, Mount Barker, I was in Port Augusta making bricks. And from there, went out with the Railways, been back up in Darwin and went down to Alice Springs and working for the DCA – Department of Civil Aviation – for a while. Well, that's going back to the '60s.

And in the Railways, like helping out on the Algebuckina Bridge. Yes, I'm sure that's correct, because that's the time I was in Dodge City and we had to go over there and give them a hand to put the new sleepers on the bridge. And from Mount Dutton, the next camp up from Dodge City, then over on the (SA) west coast; the Nullarbor; then Wirrappa – yes, moving around a lot. Kingoonya.

Coward Springs near the old Ghan narrow gauge railway. 'I've swum in there.'
(Photo courtesy of Michele Madigan)

We got that name Strangways from a bloke who was a surveyor. There are a lot of people up Marree way with that name but I never really got to meet them. I never met my father's parents. I met a couple of his brothers. Syd Strangways (Coober Pedy) could have been a cousin of my dad. In those days, you know, there were lots of Strangways.

But in my family, Johnny was the eldest – married Nancy Baker. A couple of their kids – two boys and a girl – passed on, died from asthma or something like that. Thelma was the eldest girl, married to Bernard Johnson. Their eldest son was named Tim, after our father, his grandfather. He lives somewhere in Queensland. And Ivan, the one in the mine, had a place over in Victoria – I think it was Shepparton – before he was at Prominent Hill. Then Lavina – Lavina still lives in Bundaberg. And then Nigel, he works in Canberra somewhere. I spoke to him on the phone when Lavina was here.

(Photo courtesy of Michele Madigan)

My brother Leo's first partner that I know of was Jessie Lennon; I'm not too sure – I've been away a lot. They had Judy. Leo, I think he died from alcohol. Kathy in Victoria married Walter Lang, a Scotsman. I don't think they've got any kids. Cyril – my young brother, Cyril – he died of cancer in the throat. I think he had a couple of boys – Duncan and Shane. Margaret (Wonga) is his daughter. Cyril was with one of the Johnsons there from Nepabunna – Beryl. She was related to Darryl Johnson.

Eileen's partner is Deane Willis and they've two girls and a boy – Kristie, Nicole and Eric. Her oldest children are Leanne and Melissa. Lynette is with Kevin Milera and they've got two boys, Corey and David, and two girls, Kim and Stacey.

Then me, Brian. No, never settled down with anyone – moving all the time. Yes, like I say – you've got to survive somehow.

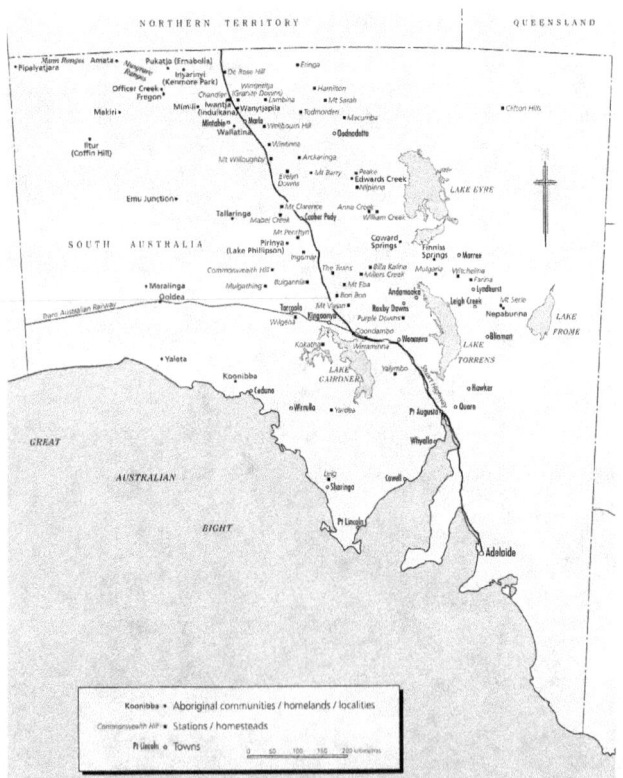

North and west of South Australia. (Umoona Community Council, Coober Pedy.

Thanks

A Coober Pedy Pioneer

Thank you very much to Michele Madigan for helping me make the book. Grateful thanks to the Institute for Aboriginal Development and Brenda Thornley for kind permission for the use of the excellent map from their publication *Yami: the autobiography of Yami Lester*; Rhonda Traeger for photo research; Nancy McLean for proofreading; Eileen Unkari Crombie for personal encouragement and support.

I Had a Good Life – It Was Beautiful

Thanks to Sister Michele Madigan (Sister Petrille) for helping make my book and to the Mary MacKillop Foundation, Sydney. Special thanks to my daughter Nellie for all her help and for her beautiful drawing of *kungari* or *kunggari*, black swan. Thanks to Mary and Mary, the printers of the first edition.

Outback Heart

Thanks to Sister Michele Madigan for having time to listen to my story and asking me questions. Without her help, this book wouldn't have been made. Thanks to my daughter Alinta. Thanks to the Mary MacKillop Foundation.

You Have To Survive Somehow

Thanks to Sister Michele Madigan, who got me started on this book, and to the Sisters of St Joseph, SA Province. Thanks also to Lynette Strangways for help with pp. 131–132.